PRAISE FOR *COACHIN*
AS A LEADER

'This book is like having a coach in your pocket for when you need it most in your work life. Whether you are looking for self-coaching in your career or want to apply coaching to how you lead a team, the authors provide practical, readily applicable coaching frameworks and approaches for leaders navigating our global, ever-changing workplace. Being a "Leader coach" is a critical mindset and skill for today that enables you to coach teams to be more resilient in the face of uncertainty, collaborate better and lead inclusively. A highly useful guide for all managers and leaders.'
Clare Russell, CEO, WDI Consulting

'Courage, compassion, curiosity and connection. The same four qualities are shared by great coaches. Here's a book that shows how to combine leadership and coaching as two sides of the same coin.'
David Clutterbuck, Practice Lead, Clutterbuck Coaching and Mentoring International

'*Coaching as a Leader* is more than a leadership book – it's a transformative guide that invites leaders to embark on a journey of self-discovery and authentic growth through the power of coaching. Rooted in deep coaching wisdom, it masterfully blends reflective practices, real-world applications and personal stories to illustrate how a coaching mindset can create meaningful impact. An essential companion for leaders committed to fostering growth within themselves, their teams and their organizations. It's not just relevant for today – it offers timeless insights for the future of leadership in our evolving world.'
Sanaz Kalantari, Organizational Coach and Leadership Development Leader, Microsoft

Coaching as a Leader

How to coach individuals and teams for improved performance

Edited by Jennifer Kidby

Association
for Coaching

KoganPage

First published in Great Britain and the United States in 2025 by Kogan Page Limited

Kogan Page

Kogan Page Ltd, 2nd Floor, 45 Gee Street, London EC1V 3RS, United Kingdom
Kogan Page Inc, 8 W 38th Street, Suite 90, New York, NY 10018, USA
www.koganpage.com

EU Representative (GPSR)

Authorised Rep Compliance Ltd, Ground Floor, 71 Baggot Street Lower, Dublin D02 P593, Ireland
www.arccompliance.com

Kogan Page books are printed on paper from sustainable forests.

© Association for Coaching International Limited, 2025

ISBNs

Hardback   978 1 3986 2118 3
Paperback   978 1 3986 2116 9
Ebook   978 1 3986 2117 6

British Library Cataloguing-in-Publication Data

A CIP record for this book is available from the British Library.

Library of Congress Control Number

2025902154

Typeset by Integra Software Services, Pondicherry
Print production managed by Jellyfish
Printed and bound by CPI Group (UK) Ltd, Croydon CR0 4YY

For leader coaches who strive to make their organization
a place where people can thrive.

CONTENTS

ABOUT THE EDITOR

Jennifer Kidby, CPsychol

Jennifer has a passion for making a difference to organizations so that they can become places for people to thrive. For over 25 years she has been applying psychology in the workplace, working with thousands of leaders in a wide range of industries as an external consultant, an internal practitioner and a leader. She knows that when work plays a positive role in people's lives, this sense of well-being ripples out into their teams, their families, their communities and beyond. She is a Chartered Psychologist, an Associate Fellow of the British Psychological Society and an accredited coach and coach supervisor. She lived and worked in the UK until 2016 when she and her family moved to Toronto, Canada for the biggest adventure of their lives. She currently works for Doane Grant Thornton LLP as the Director for Leadership Development and Succession Planning, where her role includes leading the development of a community of over 130 leader coaches across Canada. Volunteering for the Association for Coaching, offering group supervision experience calls to coaches across the world, is an important part of her professional life. She was instrumental in setting up the Executive Coaching Certificate at the University of Toronto Rotman School of Management, the first executive coaching programme in Canada to be accredited by both the Association for Coaching (AC) and the International Coaching Federation (ICF).

Jennifer currently lives in Oakville in Ontario, Canada, with her husband, daughter and two rescue cats.

FOREWORD

The world of work is undergoing a profound transformation. Organizations are navigating uncharted territories, from the evolving expectations of employees to the complexities of global challenges. In this dynamic landscape, the role of leaders has never been more critical – or more complex. Leaders are no longer simply decision-makers; they are enablers of growth, role models for collaboration and stewards of culture. It is within this context that the concept of the leader as a coach emerges not as a luxury, but as a necessity.

The Association for Coaching has long been committed to advancing coaching excellence and creating resources that inspire meaningful change. This book represents an extension of that mission. It is designed to empower leaders at all levels to harness the principles and practices of coaching, embedding them into their leadership style to drive transformation – within themselves, their teams and their organizations. A leader who adopts a coaching approach puts their focused attention on their team members and colleagues through active listening, asking powerful questions and a belief that they have the solutions within them, resulting in people feeling heard and seen. Likewise, a coaching approach encourages employees to value themselves, and others, creating higher levels of confidence to try out new approaches and ways of being.

This book brings to life a holistic and practical approach, structured into three distinct lenses: self, others and the organization, underscoring the immense potential of the leader coach mindset to create thriving, high-impact workplaces. You'll find a powerful blend of theory, lived experience and actionable strategies. Each chapter is not only a reflection of deep expertise but also a guide that equips you with the tools to begin your own journey towards coaching-inspired leadership.

As you embark on this journey, I encourage you to approach the content with an open mind and a curious heart. The practices you will explore have the power to reshape relationships, unlock potential and drive lasting impact at every level of your organization.

On behalf of the Association for Coaching, I want to thank the authors for their invaluable contributions and commitment to this important work. Together, let us champion a future where leaders are not just managers of tasks but catalysts of transformation.

Enjoy the journey.

Katherine Tulpa
CEO, Association for Coaching

ACKNOWLEDGEMENTS

I am deeply grateful to the authors and Association for Coaching team who put their trust in me to take a leap together to create this book. All are experienced coaches and leaders with different backgrounds and experiences and are driven to strengthen the culture in their organizations. Our whole-hearted thanks go to the leader coaches who inspire us and remind us about the impact this work can have.

This book was made possible by the foresight of the Association for Coaching; to see the potential of leader coaches to create an environment at work that has a positive impact on people's lives as well as business outcomes.

LIST OF CONTRIBUTORS

The creation of this book has been an act of global collaboration among our author team. We work within a wide range of industries and geographies and live across four continents. All of us are passionate about developing leader coaches in our organizations so that they can create a culture for people to be their best in their working lives and beyond. We're fortunate to get to live the culture that leader coaches are creating and have chosen to write about topics that we see make a difference in their working lives. Writing this book has been a privilege and pleasure. It's an example of what can happen when a small group of people come together with a shared vision to make a difference to organizational life. Our hope is that these pages will be useful to you as you create organizations to be places where people can thrive.

Linda Beatty

Linda holds a postgraduate certificate in executive coaching from University College Cork and is an accredited executive coach, awarded by the Association for Coaching (AC). She holds a degree in business studies and is a professional marketeer, leading the Voice of Customer programme for Bank of Ireland. In 2018 she founded and now leads the Coaching Community of Practice within Bank of Ireland, from which she set up an internal coaching faculty. Through her work leading this organically grown community of coaches she won an individual group recognition award for Enabling Colleagues to Thrive at divisional level in 2020 and at group level in 2022. Her coaching practice focuses on both professional and personal development. In her spare time, she is a member of the AC Ireland leadership team and is an enthusiastic Park Runner.

Ross Hunter

Ross is a Masters educated coach with over 20 years of experience, excelling in high-performance environments. From elite sports to consulting for start-ups, SMEs and global brands, and most recently within a FTSE 20 organization, Ross has honed his expertise across diverse settings. Early in his career, he encountered a transformative experience coaching the England Blind Cricket team. By not being blind, and unfamiliar with this version of the game, Ross discovered that effective coaching isn't about having all the answers, but about embracing curiosity and a beginner's mindset. This profound lesson became the cornerstone of his career beyond sports. As the head of coaching for a global information analytics organization, Ross played a crucial role in enhancing coaching skills among over 9,000 employees from varied cultural backgrounds. He established an internal coaching faculty of leader coaches in collaboration with the Association for Coaching. Today, Ross is deeply passionate about leveraging coaching to build high-performing teams capable of tackling humanity's most complex challenges.

Victoria Leath

Victoria is the co-founder of Leader as Coach, specializing in coaching skills training for managers, leaders and organizations. She serves as Head of Corporate Membership & Accreditation and Head of International Growth at the Association for Coaching (AC), supporting over 20 global teams, and is the founder of Inclusive Executive Coaching & Leadership Development (IECLD), specializing in leadership development. An ILM7 and AC-accredited executive coach, Victoria holds an MBA, is an Accredited PROPHET Practitioner, and combines her passion for leadership with arts and culture as a semi-professional artist. With over 25 years of international experience, she has expertise in building high-performing teams, change management, business development, marketing, and corporate governance across diverse sectors in the UK, Middle East and Europe. Known for her dynamic, creative style, Victoria's purpose is to 'inspire and stretch leaders to make a positive impact in the world'.

Katy McGregor Chartered MCIPD, ACC

Katy is a talent leader, HR business partner and an ICF credentialled coach, currently working for a global information analytics business.

She studied and lived in the UK until 2006, before moving to Sydney, Australia, where she lives today. Katy is particularly interested in building coaching capability as a vital part of the leadership toolkit, creating coaching cultures and supporting the development of under-represented talent. Passionate about contributing to the wider community, she leads the Pro Bono Coaching and Ignite Program for ICF Australasia Chapter, NSW Branch, focusing on engaging coaching for humanity and the planet, in line with the UN Sustainable Development Goals. She is also a member of the Climate Coaching Alliance and a primary ethics teacher. Her hope for the future is that the coaching community can, and will, play an integral role in addressing the most critical challenges of our times.

Nuha Al Moosa

Nuha is a Coaching Program Lead at Petroleum Development Oman, and AC-accredited foundation executive coach, driving the coaching agenda along with peer internal coaches to embed the coaching culture in day-to-day business. Her previous experiences include supporting the country in the creation of job opportunities for locals under the umbrella of In-Country Value (ICV), also known as local content talent development, enabling employees to improve their capabilities and skills while enhancing their leadership behaviours. She has also worked in the financial industry in the areas of communication, marketing, public relations and business development. Nuha studied in the American University of Sharjah, UAE, and currently lives in Muscat, Oman. She is passionate about coaching others and spreading the knowledge around behavioural coaching and its wider benefits, and aims to continue her journey in this area of expertise.

Andy Murphy

Andy is a Masters-level qualified executive coach and coach supervisor, with over 20 years' experience in leadership in the financial services industry. His enthusiasm for people development and love of coaching meant that he was chosen to help create the first internal coaching faculty for a major UK bank in 2012, which provided a template for success that has been copied across the organization.

Understanding the need to facilitate change by bringing people together he is much sought after by senior leaders and their teams, both
on an individual and group basis, who value his authentic, fun, inclusive and generative style. Passionate about building a coaching culture,
he provides executive coaching and coaching supervision to coaching
professionals on an individual and group basis. He lives in London
and is a contributing member of the Association for Coaching and the
European Mentoring and Coaching Council (EMCC).

Dena Paris

Dena is a seasoned global leader, executive coach and human resources professional. She is a certified executive coach with the
International Coaching Federation and received her coaching accreditation and training at Columbia University. Over her multi-decade
career, she has led global HR teams and functions within the professional services industry and developed deep expertise in coaching,
leadership development and talent management. In 2019 she created
and began overseeing the newly created internal executive coaching
centre of excellence within her organization and delivers individual,
group and team coaching. In 2022, Dena co-designed and began facilitating the Internal Coaching Forum for the Association for
Coaching (AC) and at the same time became a member of the AC US
leadership team. Dena is passionate about the impact coaching can
have on individuals and systems such as teams and organizations,
and strives to find ways to amplify that impact. When not working or
spending time with family and friends, she seeks out learning opportunities and life experiences that expand her thinking and understanding of the world and the people within it.

Angela Ryan FCIPD

Angela is an accomplished international HR practitioner-scholar
with a wealth of experience as a global chief human resources officer
(CHRO) in various industries and countries. She is dedicated to creating exceptional workplaces that foster individual and organizational growth and success. Angela's expertise extends to developing
internal coaching talent, believing that a coaching approach is crucial

for driving sustainable high performance and growth within organizations. With a strong background in business and a commitment to elevating the impact of HR, Angela has led HR functions in diverse organizations ranging from start-ups to large, highly regulated and listed companies. She strives not only to enhance the effectiveness of HR but also make a positive impact on the daily working lives of individuals in the organizations she serves. Angela's academic qualifications include a Doctor of Professional Studies (Human Resources), a Master of Arts in European Business, a Postgraduate Diploma in European Business Administration, and a Bachelor of Laws in European Law and Languages. She is recognized as a Chartered Fellow of the CIPD and a Fellow of the AC, showcasing her commitment to ongoing professional development and excellence in the fields of both HR and coaching.

Throughout her career, spanning over two decades and across different countries, Angela has demonstrated a passion for continuous learning, growth, and the development of both herself and those around her. Her focus on building management capabilities to be effective business leaders and coaches reflects her dedication to driving organizational success through people development and empowerment.

Paul Williamson MCIPD

Paul has over 25 years' experience working for ATG Entertainment, the world's largest live entertainment group. He has been a senior leader in sales, ticketing and HR. During his time in talent development, he has designed acclaimed in-house leadership development programmes, helped to build a successful internal coaching faculty, and coached leaders at all levels within the organization. Paul is a passionate advocate for coaching, the arts and culture, and lifelong learning. He is a Chartered Member of the CIPD and holds a Practitioner Diploma in Executive Coaching from the Academy of Executive Coaching (AoEC). Paul also specializes in coaching leaders around 'the Childhood Story', based on the work of Dr Sarah Hill and David Kantor. Paul is a member of the Regional Leadership Team, Great Britain at the Association for Coaching and has written and illustrated a book called *Pheasant Dreams*.

Tony Worgan

Tony has more than 40 years' experience as a leader in the manufacturing industry, the arts and the media. He held various leadership roles and was an editor for BBC News for many years. He also worked in the BBC's leadership development team, designing and delivering across a range of programmes. He led on coaching and mentoring for the BBC and trained many hundreds of leader coaches. He was also responsible for training, supervising and leading more than a hundred internal executive and team coaches. After leaving the BBC he became a founding partner in a consulting firm, continuing his passion for developing leader coaches. He has a Masters in Coaching Psychology and five years' training in transactional analysis.

Introduction

JENNIFER KIDBY

The power and potential of leader coaches

Leader coaches have a powerful opportunity to take coaching into every corner of their organization. Coaching skills and behaviours can transform organizational life for everyone. This is what inspired me to write this book and build a team of authors who could share their experience and guidance about how leader coaches can make a difference.

I first experienced the impact of a leader coach early in my career while I was working at the head office of a major UK bank. The head of our department was a very experienced leader who had been with the organization for many years. Once a month we had a team meeting, where he would start by asking each of us to share how we were doing and what was on our minds. Never feeling rushed or hurried, it gave an opportunity for all of us to settle into the conversation and be fully present. It set the tone. Everyone's voice was in the room regardless of seniority. Being surrounded by colleagues with more experience than me was often intimidating, but I discovered that having spoken in the opening minutes of the meeting it was easier to contribute through the rest of our time together. I felt as though I had been seen and that my perspective was welcomed, even though I believed I knew less than most of my colleagues. I felt like I belonged. Looking back on it now, and whether he knew it or not, our department head was doing what great leader coaches do – taking the skills and mindset of coaching into his everyday role as a leader.

Writing this book has encouraged me to reflect on my experience of working with leader coaches. In the years since I worked in that team I'm grateful to have worked with thousands of managers and leaders who want to bring what they've learnt about coaching into their everyday leadership. I've experienced what it's like to work alongside them as they create an environment to get the best from people, enable them tap into their potential and help them thrive at work. This book is a collaboration by authors from different industries across the world, all working within our organizations to develop leader coaches. At the time of writing all of us have internal roles in organizations, rather than being external consultants or coaches. This means that we work alongside the leader coaches we are developing. We see what works, what the challenges can be and the impact on the organization's success. In writing this book we wanted to create something that could help leaders like you take everything you know about coaching into what you do every day, so that your organization can become a place where people can be at their best and succeed in their roles.

The world needs you

The environment all of us are living and working in is significantly challenging. Global uncertainty, climate crisis, social inequality, mental health challenges, racial reckoning and growing political polarization are shaping our daily lives. As a leader coach it's likely that you're experiencing increased pressure as you try to respond to the impact of unpredictable forces in your own life while at the same time trying to connect, inspire and be vulnerable with those you lead. The World Economic Forum describes the ways leaders need to show up in this environment; to be adaptable, open to change, generate new ideas, solve problems creatively, inspire and motivate others.[1] There is a lot of paradox here; be decisive *and* flexible, be emergent *and* be action-oriented, be empathetic *and* make tough choices, be strategic *and* focus on immediate challenges. It can feel a big responsibility. The skills and flexible mindset that come with being a leader coach can help, providing a way to 'be' that embraces these challenges. It enables you to show up in ways that create inclusivity and shared prosperity through unlocking courage and leadership in all of us. That's what this book is for – to inspire and guide you to use your leader coach skills not just when you are having a formal coaching conversation, but in everyday moments.

This book is for you if:

- You are a manager or leader and want to know more about how you can bring coaching skills into your everyday role; or
- you have completed a coaching skills programme and want to learn practical ways to use what you have learnt in organizational life, beyond formal coaching; or
- you are a coach working with leaders and managers in organizations.

You'll find insights and practical guidance about how you can increase engagement and impact the performance of those around you. Simple things such as what you pay attention to in conversations, the questions you ask, your choice of words, how you begin a meeting and how you give feedback can have a big impact.

Definition of a leader coach

Throughout this book we've used the phrase 'leader coach' to describe anyone with managerial or leadership responsibility who wants to bring a coaching approach into their work. The Association for Coaching (AC) is a leading independent and not-for-profit professional body dedicated to promoting best practice and raising the awareness and standards of coaching worldwide, and it defines leader coaches as:

> those who apply a coaching mindset or coach approach to get the best out of their talent, to enable growth for future success and to achieve collective business and team performance. A leader coach inspires and enables others to adapt to constantly changing environments in ways that unleash fresh energy, innovation, and commitment. To strengthen cultures at work for future generations to thrive.[2]

Leader coaches develop skills in building trust, managing their presence, communicating effectively, raising others' awareness and insight, focusing on outcomes, holding others accountable and seeing how the wider organizational context impacts individual performance. (If you want to know more about leader coach skills, look at the AC's leader coach competency framework, www.associationforcoaching.com.)

There are many excellent books written for coaches for whom formal coaching is a core part of their professional life. As a leader coach your focus is a little different. You might engage in some formal coaching opportunities; however, success in your role is much broader than this. The focus of this book is on the opportunities you have in your everyday role. It's about the choices you make in how you behave to positively shift how others are thinking and feeling. It's in these moments that you get to touch people's lives and increase engagement and performance at work.

How to use this book

This book is structured in three parts, each looking at the role of a leader coach through a different lens.

Figure 0.1   Self, others and organization lenses

Part 1: Self lens: Focusing on you as a leader coach

The first part is about understanding and developing yourself. It's an invitation to reflect on who you are and your own development journey and how you can 'be' as a leader coach. If you know you are very action-oriented – as many leaders are – you may already be noticing an urge to skip this part to get to the 'doing' part of the book. If this is you, it's great that you already have insight into your own bias towards action. You need to consider this first lens so get comfortable with being uncomfortable! Who you are is how you lead, and that's what this first section is all about. **Chapter 1** is about your beliefs and identity, exploring questions like: Who are you as a leader coach? How do your values, beliefs and identity influence how others experience you? In what ways do your past experiences show up in your behaviour as a leader coach? It explores what it means to be present as a leader coach and the impact this has. **Chapter 2** explores a specific aspect of identity that most of us have felt at some point in our careers; being the expert who solves problems and has the right answer. The pull of expertise may be strong for you. It may be the thing that has got you to this stage in your career so far. The next step for you is to know when to let go of expertise and recognize the deeper value you can bring; helping others to improve the quality of their thinking and develop skills to find their own solutions. **Chapter 3** explores your ongoing development as a leader coach; the work you can do on yourself through self-reflection, personal growth and understanding your own reactivity.

Part 2: Others lens: Being a leader coach with employees and teams

The second part of this book is about how to bring leader coach skills into how you build relationships and lead people; the things you can pay attention to in your everyday leadership role and actions you take. You have many opportunities among your organizational responsibilities to bring coaching mindset and skills into your role. **Chapter 4** looks at elements of the employee life cycle, including recruitment, goal setting, engagement, feedback and managing performance. **Chapter 5** encourages you to listen to language; the words you use are powerful and create pictures and emotions in other people's minds. Beyond the surface structure of language is a deeper structure that conveys what's important to you and the organization. **Chapter 6** is about spotting patterns; noticing when an individual or team might be stuck in their thinking and what you can do about it. **Chapter 7** explores the opportunities you have as a team leader to create a high-performance environment for people to collaborate and bring out the best in each other.

Part 3: Organizational lens: Having impact on the organization

The third and final part focuses on going beyond one-to-one and team relationships to consider the opportunity you have for broader impact. **Chapter 8** is about formal coaching as a leader coach; if you have completed a coach development programme you may have opportunities within your organization to coach formally as part of leadership development or other engagement programmes. This is a powerful way to apply your learning and develop the next generation of leaders. Being mindful of boundaries and confidentiality is essential and is explored here. **Chapter 9** explores opportunities to strengthen your organization's culture and equip yourself with ways to bring transactional and transformational thinking into your leadership.

This book has been written to help you see the opportunities in your everyday role to apply a coaching approach. We hope you find insight and ideas among these pages so that you can strengthen your organization to be a place where people can do great work, feel they belong and make a positive contribution in the world.

References

1 Harrison, C (2022) Five rules for effective leadership in difficult times, World Economic Forum, 28 January, www.weforum.org/agenda/2022/01/five-rules-effective-leadership (archived at https://perma.cc/58AL-ETXZ)

2 Association for Coaching (2023) AC Coaching Competency Framework for Leader Coach, March, https://cdn.ymaws.com/www.association forcoaching.com/resource/resmgr/accreditation/2021_lca_docs/competency_framework_-_leade.pdf (archived at https://perma.cc/LFX8-THPG)

PART ONE
Self lens

Focusing on you
as a leader coach

Organization lens:
Having an impact on the
organization

Others lens:
Being a leader coach with
employees and teams

Self lens:
Focusing
on you as a
leader
coach

Who am I?   1

PAUL WILLIAMSON

Who am I? Three small words.

On the surface, a question easily answered. You could just give your name after all. If the question was repeated, then what? What would you say next? You've given your name, and you open your mouth, and you say 'I am...'. It's an important question to explore, knowing yourself well is essential for being an effective leader coach. Your core values, beliefs, drivers and derailers all influence how you show up in the moment and the impact you have on others. Having a deep level of awareness of your inner world equips you to be an authentic and compassionate leader, prepared to show passion, vulnerability and humanity. A clear sense of who you are as a leader coach also enables you to better articulate your vision and purpose. When you can do this, you are much more likely to enhance collaboration within teams, aligning people around a shared mission, creating a greater sense of belonging and giving clarity. Being authentic creates trust within a team and enhances your credibility and influence. This can have a tangible impact on the willingness of team members to engage openly and contribute at their very best. This, in turn, impacts positively on things like talent retention, innovation and productivity.

In uncertain times of volatility and change, knowing yourself provides a stable foundation from which you can move with greater agility. You can adapt strategies when required while also staying true to your values. This provides you and those you lead with a sense of stability at the heart of things, which is enabling and generative during times of flux. Knowing yourself well as a leader coach and being curious about how your lived experience has helped to shape you opens the door to greater empathy and connection with others. Those three simple words, 'Who am I?' repeated again and again have the power to reveal a great deal.

Digging deeper – a framework

To guide you through a process of self-reflection, I'm going to introduce a framework that acknowledges the layers that contribute to a sense of who you are.

To illustrate the various stages of enquiry, I'm going to use a metaphor. Imagine a tree. This tree represents public-facing you – the version of you that is seen by others. It encompasses your appearance, speech and the stories you share, alongside your actions and behaviours. Just as a tree is shaped by the elements around it, you are influenced by your environment – its challenges, stresses and rewards, all of which will affect you and generate a reaction or emotional response.

As in the diagram in Figure 1.1, below the surface, the tree has roots that reach down through the earth. Just like the layers in the earth itself, there are layers of meaning that exist associated with who you are. These layers, when examined, explain what constitutes 'you' and why you show up the way you do. The important point to remember with this line of enquiry is that the majority of these layers are unseen. Furthermore, the elements within these layers, the tectonic plates of your lived experience if you like, move, and can create a reaction on the surface when activated. The effects on the surface can be benign, encourage creativity, connection and growth, or can be far more destructive, causing conflict, damage and isolation. The implications of this are far-reaching. If unexamined, adverse behavioural patterns may play out and create a harmful environment 'up top' on the surface. If you don't do the required work on yourself, you may unwittingly negatively influence the work systems you are a part of and contribute to an unhealthy or 'toxic' work environment, which is another reason why this work is so important.

Figure 1.1   Digging deeper framework

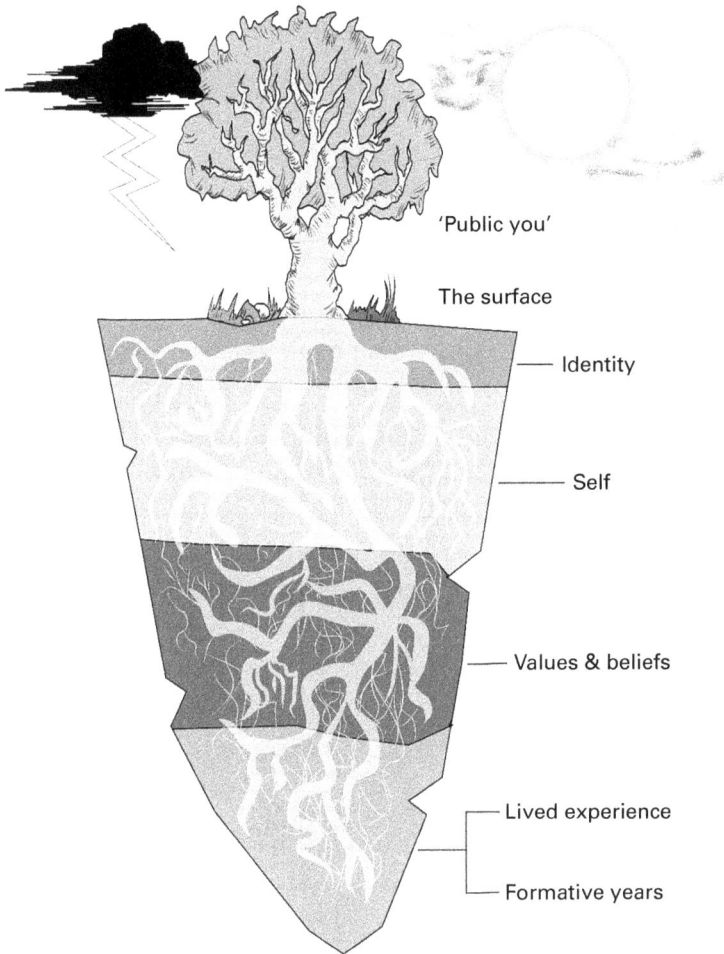

'Public you'

The surface

Identity

Self

Values & beliefs

Lived experience

Formative years

At the deepest level we have our lived experience and formative years, our 'childhood stories', which influence old internal narratives that we carry into adulthood. Our lived experience continues from childhood into adulthood and from this we develop our values and beliefs at the next layer. This is influenced by the various systems we are a part of and provides us with our guiding principles that we return to time and time again. Above this, our sense of self develops – our personality traits, abilities, likes and dislikes populate this layer. Here we get a sense of what motivates and fulfils us as well as what doesn't. It is where our self-esteem resides, and where our personal needs might sit. The top layer is 'identity', which we may show to the outside world through our affiliations and our outward expression of self. This layer is also influenced by how we think others might see us.

Having taken an initial look at the framework we'll now examine some of the layers in more detail, starting on the surface.

The surface – 'public you'

The surface, or public you, is what people see, hear and notice about you. It influences how others experience you. Within the world of business, we are increasingly aware of branding. Just as we might ask ourselves what makes a great brand, you might also ask 'what's my brand of leadership?' The degree to which a brand becomes successful is determined by how well it connects with customers in its market. Similarly, success as a leader coach will be decided by the degree to which you can connect, coach and inspire your people to perform at their best. In many respects, answering the question 'who am I?' is the beginning of a process to understand your own personal brand, and what parts of you can enable, or suppress, growth and engagement within a team.

Take a moment to think of a successful brand.

- What do you notice about that brand?
- What comes to mind when you think about that brand?
- Is it clear what they do and why they do it?

Chances are that the brand is very clear about who they are and what they stand for. People know what to expect, and choose whether to follow, trust and buy from the brand. Daniel Goleman made a similar observation in connection with leadership, when he wrote about 'resonant leadership' in his book *Primal Leadership*.[1] He argued that leaders who demonstrate a high degree of emotional intelligence are much more likely to create resonance and harmony within teams and across an organization.

Identity

In this framework the first level beneath the surface is identity and speaks to the 'social face'; how you think you are seen by others. Like all of us, you play many different roles in life, to some of which you will naturally attach greater meaning, according to your preferences and talents. With reference to the framework we're using here, this layer appears near the surface because our various identities can often be seen by others, or their influence can be detected in our words, actions and behaviours. The tree analogy, with its complicated network of roots, is deliberately used to convey the idea that what may appear near the surface may have its roots much further down in the layers beneath, going right back to our formative years. An exploration of identity forms part of the answer to who you are and is therefore a good place to start.

ACTIVITY
Exploring identity

1   Let's begin quite broadly. Make a list of various descriptors you would assign to yourself. This could include things like your name, height, ethnicity, nationality, etc.

2   Next, make a list of the various roles you play in life, e.g., a parent, sibling, writer, athlete, blogger, friend, analyser, adventurer, etc.

3   What descriptors and roles stand out for you? Notice how you feel about each item on your list. Do some hold a different energy? Do some of the items trigger thoughts, memories, emotions? For example, just your name may trigger some interesting associations – do you like your name? Have you ever had a nickname? Growing up, did people abbreviate or elongate your name? What meaning might you attribute to this? What did this create in you?

4   Thinking about your list, some of the identities you've noted down might feel more significant than others. Take a step back mentally to consider them as they appear on the page. Those that hold energy for

you are likely to influence you more 'in the moment' and potentially show up in your leadership too. If we take the identity of being a parent as an example, if you are a parent yourself, you may be drawn strongly to this identity. Thinking about this more deeply, you may recognize that aspects of this identity show up when you're leading at work. You may tend to protect team members, like you would your own children for example, or rescue them when difficulty arises, or offer advice, whether it's asked for or not.

Once formed, it's tempting to believe our identity is fixed. Certainly, some aspects of our identity remain with us throughout our lives, such as our race or nationality, but our relationship to these identities may alter over the years. Major life events and upheavals like divorce, ill health, relocation, change of career or retirement can lead us to explore and redefine our identities in light of the changes that have happened. With this in mind, it is helpful to consider how your identity may have shifted and changed over time and accept that this is likely to continue as you grow older.

Self

The next layer in the framework is self. Digging deeper invites you to explore your personality, abilities, likes and dislikes to raise your self-awareness, which is vital for a leader coach. Understanding your preferences and motivations and how they impact others is a key part of being effective. There are numerous personality and behavioural profiling tools available that can help in this regard. These profiles can provide valuable insight and go a long way to bring into focus aspects of self that can help or hinder you as a leader coach. Combined with coaching they can provide an excellent foundation for personal development.

The other benefit of digging deeper is that greater self-awareness allows you to access greater authenticity, which ultimately will enhance your impact as a leader coach. A good first step is understanding your drivers and 'why you do what you do'.

ACTIVITY
Why you do what you do

1 Think about things you have a natural aptitude for. What are you good at? Note them down. They may not necessarily be things you love doing, but you may have been told by other people you're good at them. Notice the energy each thing on the list holds for you.

2 Building on this, now write a list of things you are most passionate about, your interests – it could be exercise, music, cooking, team sports, languages, travel, etc.

3 Look out for things that are repeated across each of your lists, or themes running between them. These aspects are likely to heavily influence who you are today and how you show up.

4 Reflect on the themes you have identified by writing expressively to deepen your reflection. The key to writing 'expressively' is to let go of self-censorship, forget about spelling, grammar and neatness, in favour of a stream of consciousness. This type of writing, pioneered by the social psychologist James Pennebaker, has been proven to have several surprising benefits (everything from building stronger immune systems to improving the quality of your sleep).[2] In this context, as you write, notice any themes that emerge as you explore who you are.

Values and beliefs

Digging deeper, arriving at the next layer, one might ask 'what values and beliefs sit behind my identity and sense of self?' Understanding how these inform how you show up, behave and make decisions is vital as a leader coach. Sometimes these are very clear, other times they might be present but more unconscious. One way to access and clarify your underlying values and beliefs is to look back and remember key moments in your life, where these have been learnt and set down. It is worth examining these moments in more detail and mining them for insight into your core values.

ACTIVITY

Surfacing values and beliefs

1 Recall a story from your lived experience about a significant event that continues to hold meaning for you. It doesn't necessarily have to be an extraordinary event; sometimes the most profound moments can be quite small and low-key. The important thing is that it is a memory that feels significant to you and has influenced who you are today. Examples might be a story about an important life-lesson, a turning point, a time of change, a big decision, a moment of truth, a realization.

2 Write your story expressively. Take your time. Write fulsomely, recalling as much detail as you can. Once you have finished, take a break and return to it later to read through.

3 As you read back what you have written, notice the language you have used. Are there words that are repeated? Do some of them feel charged in any way? What themes emerge from the story? Notice how you feel reading it back. Which sections of the story resonate with you most, and why?

4 The story you've chosen may reveal some interesting aspects of your personality and your belief system. What values and beliefs are detectable in the story? Things you believe in, which help you stay true to yourself? The story you have chosen is likely to yield at least one core value. Now consider what else feels important to you from other life experiences you have encountered. Try to identify between four and six core values. Wherever possible try to capture each value in one or two words.

One important point to make in relation to your values is that these are principles you want to commit to living your life by. Being ruled by one core value could be deeply problematic, leading to a dogmatic approach that is not inclusive. The power in having a range of values allows you to find balance and provide the right degree of agility to face challenges and issues that arise. For example, having a value around valuing 'self-expression' above all else could be taken too far if it leads you to assert that your view of the world, and all your ideas, are sacrosanct and cannot be challenged. If, however, you had a second core value about 'celebrating difference' these two values would work in concert, allowing you to welcome and appreciate different forms of self-expression and be more inclusive.

Having started to explore the layers of meaning related to who you are, let's now look at an example and see how reactions at the various layers can manifest for someone else. The examples in this chapter are inspired by real people, but some elements have been changed or stories adapted and merged to anonymize the individuals involved and encourage your own reflections.

From an early age, Alan was passionate about making things. At school he was told he was 'good with his hands' and encouraged to focus on practical subjects, as his performance in more academic subjects was weaker than that of most of his peers. After leaving school, he joined the construction industry via an apprenticeship scheme, and through hard work and application, quickly established himself as a talented and well-regarded trainee. When the apprenticeship ended, he was given a permanent position. He proved himself to be a great technician and impressed his managers with the speed, efficiency and quality of his work. He loved learning from more experienced team members, felt a great deal of gratitude to those early mentors and knew he wanted to 'give back' in some way in the future. The only way to do this was to become a manager himself. He felt extremely nervous about making the transition and knew that he would need to let go of much of the fulfilling work he had built his reputation on, in favour of leading a team of people who would carry out most of the practical work. He was also aware that an old internal narrative from his school days about 'not being intelligent enough' was playing in the background and contributing to a feeling of inferiority. He felt that people expected managers to have all the answers and be able to manage with authority and certainty. It was a difficult transition. Initially, Alan felt his identity as a skilled technician was being eroded/lost, and his approach to his team felt clumsy and mannered. Fortunately, he was offered some coaching with an internal coach who encouraged him to reflect on his career journey. From this he was able to identify positive core values and beliefs that sat behind his story. He recognized that he took real pride and satisfaction from building things, had always been curious, loved learning, and possessed a real desire to develop people and build on their potential, believing that inside everyone was a talent for something. These themes were all authentic to him and the coaching allowed him to reframe his current experience in an enabling way. If he used his curiosity and love of learning to build connection and coach his line reports, he could build trust and develop a high-performing team. The same feelings of pride and satisfaction could be achieved by creating a safe, nurturing environment where learning was valued, and contribution encouraged and celebrated.

Take a moment to reflect on Alan's story. If you were to recount your career journey to date, what themes might emerge? Use the questions below to prompt further reflection and note down your responses.

- What is/has been your identity in the workplace, past and present? How and why has this evolved?

- How well did/do these identities serve you?

- What beliefs sit behind some of the decisions you've made regarding your career?

- Have you ever been influenced by other people's desires and expectations, or the beliefs and traditions laid down in a system? How?

- What have been the major transitions in your career journey and what did you learn from these experiences?

- What were your beliefs about leadership when you started work? Where did these come from? How well have these beliefs served you?

Sometimes there can be a strong pull towards a line of work, which can go very deep. Alan's story highlights how the work that you do can form part of how you define yourself. In his case it was centred around being 'good with his hands', and the value of being skilled and practical – building things. When he moved into a leadership position, this identity was challenged and required adaptation.

Alan's experience also highlights how we are often shaped and influenced by the system we are a part of. Alan's sense of self was influenced by his experience of the schooling system he was part of and what his teachers told him during his formative years.

Lived experiences and formative years

Lived experiences and formative years is the deepest layer in our framework. Systems play a big part in how we make sense of who we are. For most of us, our family is the first system we're a part of. Our place in the family, what is rewarded and what is punished, what elicits praise and what generates disapproval, all has an impact on our development. If you go right back to the beginning and consider your name, this is the first big statement of 'who you are' and it's given to you by your family system. You do not choose your name – it's given to you. You may have been given the name of an ancestor, a favourite place, famous person, an important association, or given a name which holds some symbolic meaning for the person that chose it. Such stories are absorbed into an understanding of who you are. What stories exist for you?

An important reason for doing this kind of deeper work on yourself is that the world of work has changed significantly. As younger generations of people enter the workplace, their expectations of what a leader (and the organization) should provide are different from the past. In the modern workplace, leaders are now expected to create psychologically safe, inclusive environments where people can be themselves – speak, be heard and contribute. This requires leaders to demonstrate high levels of EQ (emotional intelligence), the first element of which is self-awareness. If demonstrated, this has the potential to transform an organization's culture. A key concept in creating an inclusive environment for all is the requirement to recognize that everyone has a different 'lived experience'.

Your lived experience will have profoundly influenced you and contributed to who you are today. Some of this you may carry with you front and centre, and be very aware of; other aspects may be more unconscious, but no less important. Surfacing this, contextual-izing it, and understanding how your lived experience might influence how you show up as a leader coach, and crucially, how this impacts on those that you lead, is vital if you want to lead successfully in the modern world. Author and coach Salma Shah explores this in her book *Diversity, Inclusion and Belonging in Coaching* and notes:

> Behind every one of us is our lived experience: a childhood, cultural, socio-economic, religious and gender identity and a systemic ancestral story that can inspire us to achieve greatness, act with compassion, be resilient and make a difference. Yet our lived experience can also wreak havoc, cause self-sabotage, contribute towards our playing small and leave us lacking the confidence to be authentic.[3]

Returning to the framework, our roots below the surface spread out widely and are sometimes entangled with the various systems we have encountered within our lived experience, from childhood right up until the present day. Alan's story demonstrates how a person's actions and behaviours on the surface are influenced by the layers that lie beneath. Our roots, which stretch right down to our forma-tive years, can send ripples right up to the surface, which get ex-pressed in actions and behaviours that are observable by others. So, when Alan was first promoted, he felt like an imposter. His childhood story about not being intelligent enough was activated and his new job challenged a historic narrative about only being able to find value and purpose in practical, technical work. This internal conflict ini-tially prompted him to withdraw, doubt himself and appear clumsy in his approach, which generated dissonance rather than resonance within the team he was leading. By expanding his view and recogniz-ing positive, authentic aspects of who he was, Alan was able to re-frame his current reality and introduce a new internal narrative that served him better as a leader and still felt authentic.

Our childhood stories

Childhood is longer than most people think. Developmentally we don't reach full adulthood until our early twenties. Our 'formative years' are called that for a good reason – this time forms us and influences a good deal of how we show up in adulthood.

In her book *Where Did You Learn to Behave Like That?* Dr Sarah Hill explores the power and impact of our childhood stories, the source of so many of our more problematic reactions and behaviour.[4] Hill explains how things that happened to us during our formative years, and our experience of 'imperfect love', lead us to construct internal narratives that we return to in adulthood. These old narratives are laid down in childhood and revisited so frequently they become default positions generating patterns of behaviour. Not all of these serve us well. It is in high-stakes situations we are most likely to see problematic reactions and behaviour being triggered. This kind of high-stakes reactivity can be very damaging and cause harm – to self, individuals, teams and reputation. In organizational life, the more senior a person becomes, the more likely these reactive behaviours go unchallenged, which sometimes results in an unhealthy culture developing, so the negative impact can be far-reaching.

Let's look at an example of this in action. Imagine for a moment you have a childhood story where you were ridiculed by a teacher in front of a class, which prompted further derision and laughter from your peers who then teased you. This story led you to create an internal narrative which said, 'I am stupid, and people will never take me seriously'. Now, in adulthood, you're presenting to a team at work about a project you're leading on. You notice two people at the back of the room whispering and laughing. You stop presenting, shout at the individuals concerned and then storm out of the meeting room.

In this example, feelings of inadequacy and anger are ignited in the moment. The child in you feels angry at being mocked, lashes out and then, overcome with shame, runs away. The work to be done here would be to examine the old internal narrative through an adult's eyes. While the childhood story itself is immutable (the facts of what happened in our formative years cannot be altered), one can find compassion for that hurt child. The harsh statements that the child created that have been carried into adulthood (the old internal narrative) can then be systematically challenged and repurposed. So, in the example cited, you could begin by gathering factual evidence that discounts the statement 'I am stupid, and people will never take me seriously'. Examples where you have overcome difficult problems, been promoted, been chosen for something or given additional responsibility would be powerful and tangible examples that challenge the old narrative and point towards a positive alternative. The process of discovering a new, enabling internal narrative is described in Dr Sarah Hill's book and is well worth exploring.

Again, returning to our framework, this example demonstrates how our roots at the deepest layer (our formative years) can be shaken, sending tremors up through the layers, resulting in negative behaviour and unmoderated emotional responses being enacted on the surface, which is observable by others, resulting in potential reputational damage.

This kind of experience is remarkably commonplace. Have you ever witnessed a leader overreact to something in a meeting? Someone asks an innocuous question, or makes a comment that sparks an emotional reaction that seems out of proportion, and you witness a dramatic emotional display. Maybe this is something you know you've done yourself. You will know the kind of event I'm talking about, as it's likely to make you wince when you recall it. Chances are, when people react in this way, a childhood story has entered the room. That seemingly innocuous comment or question has triggered an (often subconscious) association with a person, event or situation from childhood. If this happens to you in a meeting, you react as the child, in a way that makes sense to that child. You may have a tantrum, or pound the desk in frustration, or burst into tears, or march out and slam the door, or totally shut down and do and say nothing at all, when perhaps, it's a time where you're needed most.

Old internal narratives can restrict us, narrow our perspective and prevent us from reaching our full potential. Let's look at how another manager was negatively influenced by an old internal narrative, and how they found a way to expand their repertoire of responses and explore a new, positive internal narrative that served them and their team far better.

Chris worked in a busy marketing team. The workload was heavy, and the pace of the business was fast. Chris was driven to achieve results and had perfectionistic tendencies. They didn't fully trust their team and the pressure to inspect their work and maintain a high-quality output was exhausting. They had a very low tolerance for mistakes and tended to micromanage anyone who failed to deliver to their standards. Some of this was driven by fear and fuelled by a childhood story that involved a great deal of insecurity, threat and instability. Their quest for predictability and control felt like the only way to avoid feeling as small and as powerless as they had done growing up in their family system. Overwhelmed and tired, they reached out to their coach.

During a session with their coach, Chris was asked to think of a time where they felt relaxed, in the moment and 'in tune' with people around them. Chris instantly recalled a happy time in their youth when they attended a dance school. They described the feeling of absolute freedom when everyone had learnt a routine and moved with ease and fluidity. Their memory was that everything in that moment felt effortless and graceful. They just tuned in, listened to the music, the rhythm, their fellow dancers, and everything flowed. Chris's coach asked them to identify what contributed to this feeling of being in flow. Chris said they had listened, trusted themselves and knew in that moment that they could dance – there had been no self-doubt. They trusted their fellow dancers, tuned in to their energy and pace and matched them. Chris's coach reflected that they had lit up when describing this memory – their body language had become visibly more relaxed and far more expressive. Chris's coach also asked them to look back and recall what happened leading up to that dance performance. Chris talked about a rehearsal process, which was challenging but fun. At the beginning, it was messy, everyone made mistakes as they learnt the routine. They were all in the same boat though, all vulnerable, learning as they went along, patiently trying out new things. They experimented with different choreography until they found what worked. The coach then asked Chris to consider what they could take from this joyful memory and apply in their current situation. Were there parts of themselves they hadn't let free in the workplace that might help?

Harnessing the free-spirited, creative and resourceful side of themselves, Chris was able to change their energy and focus. When they met with their team, they tuned in, asked questions, and really listened to their thoughts and contributions. Chris quickly discovered that as they relaxed, the team did too. Creating a challenging but fun environment for the work to take place, where mistakes could happen and be learnt from, led to greater confidence and improved performance. People began to thrive, delivering far more innovative work and achieving incredible results, as trust and connection within the team blossomed.

Take a moment to reflect on Chris's story. Does it resonate with you? Can you recall times in the past where you've felt a sense of being 'in flow'? A time where you were in your element?

- What were you doing when you felt 'in flow'?
- Where were you? Who were you with?
- How did you feel, both physically and emotionally?
- What does this tell you?
- If someone was observing you 'in flow', what qualities would they see in you?
- Do you use these qualities when you are leading? If not, could you? If you are, how could you build on them?

Within our framework, answering these questions will allow you to return to the layer related to 'self'. Reflecting further around this to explore what motivates (and demotivates) you will yield more insight. You'll notice that emerging themes will present themselves and these will give you a greater understanding of what needs to be present in your life and work, for you to feel fulfilled. If attended to fully, you will not only raise your self-awareness but also experience greater self-esteem. You'll also notice from the example given here, that by identifying a story from their formative years, Chris was able to access an authentic part of themselves that they had hitherto not brought to work. This insight led to a new more empowering internal narrative and core values that strengthened creativity, learning and collaboration.

Having explored the various layers, returning one final time to our framework, it is important to recognize that you are continually growing, just like a tree, and life and all the experiences it has to offer will continue to stimulate, influence and change you. A key feature of being a leader coach is adopting a growth mindset. This philosophy favours curiosity over dogmatic certainty. It welcomes in the contributions of others and creates a psychologically safe environment where people can thrive in the workplace. This contrasts sharply with the fixed mindsets so often experienced in corporate life. It counteracts the belief that you are restricted and kept in your place by limitations.

With this in mind, your answer to the question 'who am I?' will change too. You are multifaceted. You are flexible. You are capable of many things. Revisiting the question 'who am I?' from time to time is therefore highly recommended. It is also true to say that the more we are ourselves, paradoxically, the more we are likely to grow, develop and change.

> Be more of who you are – work with the flow, adapting and accepting yourself as you are.[5]

Digging deeper into who you are generates greater confidence. It allows you to find and maintain a stable core within yourself, enabling you to take on new challenges. One of the biggest challenges facing a leader coach is letting go of technical expertise and that's what we'll be exploring in Chapter 2. Then, rounding off the first section of the book, in Chapter 3 you'll hear an inspiring real-life story about ongoing development as a leader coach and lifelong practice.

References

1 Goleman, D, Boyatzis, R and McKee, A (2004) *Primal Leadership: Learning to lead with emotional intelligence*, Harvard Business School Press, Boston, MA

2 Pennebaker, J and Evans, J (2014) *Expressive Writing: Words that heal*, Idyll Arbor, Enumclaw, WA

3 Shah, S (2022) *Diversity, Inclusion and Belonging in Coaching: A practical guide*, Kogan Page, London

4 Hill, S (2017) *Where Did You Learn to Behave Like That?: A coaching guide for working with leaders*, Dialogix

5 Leary-Joyce, J (2014) *The Fertile Void: Gestalt coaching at work*, AoEC Press, St Albans

Letting go of expertise

2

ROSS HUNTER AND KATY MCGREGOR

It is said that who we are is how we lead and coach. In Chapter 1 you explored the question of 'who am I?' – the layers of experience, values and beliefs, identity and narratives that drive your behaviour. You considered that the answer to this question will constantly change as you grow and experience new things that shape your identity. In this chapter we'll take this further by considering expertise and its place in your role and identity as a leader coach. We'll invite you to reflect on what technical expertise means to you, the value it has for others, and how and when to share it in service of your colleagues and organization.

First, let's consider the role of a leader. While there is no one single definition of what a leader is, most models include a similar list of traits, capabilities and some level of expertise. Your expertise has been gained through your life, education and career experiences to date. You may find yourself using and sharing it differently at certain points in your career, depending on your role, goals and position within your organization, as well as what your colleagues need from you.

This leads us to a paradox you'll have no doubt encountered as a leader coach. Technical expertise is the very element that you have been promoted and recognized for. Maybe it's what members of your team are asking for or expecting from you. Letting go of that, even holding it more lightly, can be very challenging and is also an incredible opportunity. While your expertise is what earned you recognition and promotion, and it's often what your team seeks or expects from you, the paradox lies in the fact that relying too heavily on it can sometimes limit your effectiveness. Letting go of the need to always be the expert, or even approaching it with a lighter touch, can be challenging, but it also opens up the possibility for greater growth and collaboration within your team.

Why let go of expertise?

There will be different elements to your technical expertise, gained through your career, including skills, knowledge and experience. There will also be expertise gained through your broader life, for example, knowledge and experiences that have shaped how you make decisions, your ability to deal with change, your attitude, behaviours and mindset. Leader coaches make deliberate choices about when and how to share the expertise they have acquired through their life.

Take a moment to reflect on your thoughts and feelings about how you share expertise.

- What feelings come up for you when you think of your expertise? What do you notice?
- How has the way you use your expertise changed throughout your career?
- How tightly or lightly do you hold your expertise when leading and coaching today?
- How do you feel about letting go of your expertise?

Finally, how are the values and beliefs you have about leadership showing up in your reflections? You may like to note down your insights at this stage and come back to them later to see what has shifted for you as you explore this topic further.

The shifting landscape for leader coaches

To understand why leader coaches sometimes choose to let go of their expertise, we'll start with the bigger picture. The world is shifting rapidly. Social, environmental and geopolitical landscapes are changing faster than ever before, and with this backdrop a leader's role is also changing. Many leaders are navigating the complexity of managing multiple generations in the same team, perhaps they are also working with rapidly evolving new technology. Leaders are also being challenged to think about how and where work is done, the size and shape of their teams and how to be more sustainable in their work practices.

Take a moment to think about what you're now being called to do and deliver as a leader. There are likely to be performance targets that clearly set out 'what' success looks like – the numbers, the deliverables, the strategy. This isn't new. However, to be considered a successful leader today you are also now accountable for 'how' this outcome is achieved. This is the change. The people-related targets, behaviours and culture, and the engagement of your team are likely to be part of your success. This is where coaching has a big impact for you, your team, the organization and your wider stakeholders.

Leadership development experts Jack Zenger and Joe Folkman conducted research into leadership strengths and their impact: 'When it comes to improving productivity, employee engagement, retention, employee development, and supervisor performance, there is simply no better activity than having a leader who coaches and develops their direct reports regularly.'[1] They also note that it's a skill everyone can learn. While not easy or a quick fix, this shows that a coaching approach – as opposed to being overly directive – can have a significant impact.

Achieving these important outcomes means using thoughtful questions, listening and empathy to explore somebody else's ideas and solutions. This helps them to reach their own conclusions and find their own way. We love this summary, shared by a leader coach in our organization who described their role as 'build the best road possible, so whatever the car that is on that road it has the best chance to perform at its best'.

Consider the individual, organizational and societal expectations of those you lead today. A leader coach in China shared her powerful journey to coaching, connecting history, culture and educational philosophies with new challenges and expectations.

Confucianism is a culture that the Chinese nation has been pursuing for more than 2,000 years, having a great impact on the formation of the national character and Chinese society. It emphasizes the supremacy of ethics and morality, respect for teachers and filial piety (to be good to one's parents). I was born in the 1970s and have been a manager more than 20 years. I was taught from a young age to unconditionally obey my parents at home, teachers at school, and leaders at work. When learning and embracing the philosophy of coaching, my challenge was how to overcome the idea of ethical supremacy.

While we have not all grown up in Confucian cultures, we are all influenced in some way by our education, the approaches of parents and teachers, and the organizational systems we have been part of. In reflecting on our own influences, we might consider how expertise was valued. How did our role models use their expertise? How were questions perceived, particularly from and by those in authority? This leader coach went on to share how this is evolving.

This challenge is much smaller for managers younger than me, because they grew up in a more open society with more diverse ideas after China's reform and opening up… Today's world is undergoing unprecedented rapid change and uncertainty. It has made me and my peers realize that our past experience does not solve the new problems we face today. Traditional concepts and management models cannot meet these needs, and coaching has become the most effective concept and method for managers.

This leader coach ended by sharing the notion of 'warming the past and learning the new', which summarizes beautifully the idea of valuing and sometimes using experience, at the same time as evolving and embracing new behaviours and ways of being.

Like the leader coach quoted above, you might also operate in complex organizational systems, in multigenerational teams, and across cultures. You might be finding there are limits to the value that your expertise can bring in a world that is rapidly changing. What your colleagues need from you might be changing too. While there are many commonalities across the generations, research shows that Generation Y (or Millennials) are looking for more coaching and feedback from their leaders. In her *Harvard Business Review* article 'Millenials want to be coached at work' Karie Willyerd notes 'conversations with hundreds of Millennials made it clear that what they want most from their managers isn't more managerial direction, per se, but more help with their own personal development.'[2] She also notes the importance of leadership authenticity by sharing personal stories of successes and failures – perhaps this is the evolution of how we have previously thought about sharing our expertise.

We propose that applying experience and expertise is simply not as important or effective as it once was. Today's challenges in organizations are different and often more complex. They require solutions that perhaps have not yet been conceived. For many organizations the ability to innovate and adapt will be their source of competitive advantage, not how much expertise they hold. In our organization, leader coaches are now applying coaching to innovation and the process of testing ideas to achieve just that – it's exciting to imagine the possibilities.

The powerful pull of technical expertise

We have all experienced a powerful pull to tell someone what we think they should do. Why might that be? It feels good? It helps others? You're expected to give the answer? It is deeply connected to your belief about the value you bring at work, as you explored in Chapter 1. You are likely to have started your career as an individual contributor with years of honing your craft. It's a common journey which builds a solid foundation of expertise and knowledge. You understand how to perform and to give the best of yourself.

A senior director in a product development division shared this reflection with us.

In many of my previous roles, finding the answer to a problem was time sensitive. When critical components of our key business machinery, which demanded availability, reliability and performance, suddenly became unavailable, my job function was to get people together, find the solution and to do it quickly.

This highlights the high-pressure environment in which they operated, where quick problem-solving was crucial. The urgency of the situation often dictated a rapid (perhaps default) response.

Consequently, when I came to coaching, my conditioned reflex to jump straight into the solution space was overly pronounced. I was immediately directive, offering advice, providing guidance and giving instruction.

Here, they acknowledge the challenge of transitioning from a problem-solving mindset to a coaching approach. The instinct to provide immediate solutions can be hard to overcome, especially when they are used to being the go-to expert.

I was certain to be able to find a solution for them. Surely they know how experienced I am? And, perhaps worst of all, why is this all taking so long?

There is an internal struggle and impatience that can arise when shifting from a directive to a coaching role. This director's confidence in their expertise led to frustration when the coaching process seemed slow.

I was missing the point. I didn't recognize my own arrogance. I wasn't seeing the value within the individual.

Finally, this realization underscores a critical insight: effective coaching requires recognizing and valuing the individual's potential, rather than simply providing answers. This shift in perspective is essential for fostering growth and collaboration.

As the example above shows, the term 'knowledge is power' is ingrained in us. We are taught through education, exams and benchmarking that knowing the answer is favoured. It feels good to have the right answer and in turn to give this to someone else. There is a surge in the release of adrenaline and dopamine in our brain. It feels powerful. This creates a tension, as a member of our organization summarized, 'I really value coaching but it just feels so good to be able to give the answer.'

Michael Bungay Stanier puts this in perspective in his book *The Advice Trap*, encouraging us to tame our advice monsters.[3] Our monster may have a preference to Tell-it, Save-it or Control-it, but in whatever guise they show up, he notes that they 'all share the same DNA, a core belief you hold in that moment when your advice monster is loose: You're better than the other person.' This may be hard to accept, surely we don't think like that? That our advice positions us as better than others? However, if you pause and reflect, you'll see the uncomfortable truth in this.

As a leader coach you may be considering and appreciating the way power dynamics shift when you step into a coaching approach, from having 'power over' someone, to sharing 'power with' them or giving 'power to' them through your actions. The image of the advice monster is perhaps a good one to keep in mind when the temptation to give advice comes up for you. What does yours look, sound and feel like?

Discomfort and growth

Part of the Association for Coaching's leader coach definition is that 'a leader coach inspires and enables others to adapt to constantly changing environments in ways that unleash fresh energy, innovation, and commitment. To strengthen cultures at work for future generations to thrive.' As you grow as a leader coach, you'll naturally start to broaden the range of areas you coach on and people you coach within this context of constant change. As you are gradually letting go of a reliance on sharing expertise, you may feel a sense of discomfort or disruption to your leadership identity. You might particularly notice this when coaching around new or complex topics. This could also show up when you feel stuck without an obvious solution or goal to work towards that will solve the challenge for the coachee; perhaps your advice now seems insignificant in the face of the challenge.

Let's imagine for a minute you're coaching a member of your team and they bring up a challenge they've been grappling with between a commercial decision and their strong personal value of living sustainably. When faced with bigger questions the act of advice giving simply won't get us very far, nor does it demonstrate respect for the coachee in bringing an issue of importance into the conversation. You may have already encountered such situations. This can be uncomfortable, we may feel like moving away from the conversation, or making it smaller so that we feel more in control. Charly Cox, author of *Climate Change Coaching*, notes 'Many of us have been socialized to offer advice... We also want to be helpful, or perhaps we find the very idea of being stuck a bit terrifying.'[4] This is also our opportunity to grow.

As you continue your journey as a leader coach it's important to continue to self-reflect, as well as develop your skills and expertise. You'll benefit from doing the inner work we often neglect, to explore and identify where your approach has a deeper driver, or unmet need. For example, noticing if you feel your self-worth is tied to the knowledge and expertise that you have, and share.

Your reflections on not knowing the answers

Consider your own relationship with uncertainty and not knowing all the answers. Reflect on how this plays out in your conversations and leadership.

- In your role, what patterns do you notice about the topics you're coaching on most often?
- What does it feel like to lead when you don't have expertise – compared to when you do?
- What are you learning about yourself from this reflection?

When might expertise be useful?

Let's look at the other side of this equation. How may expertise be helpful, when used in the right way, deliberately and mindfully? As a leader coach you're likely to be time pressured, coaching in the flow of work, with multiple priorities competing for your attention. Here's where expertise can help, by enabling you to go to the core of the issue, narrowing the right questions to ask. It can be a valuable short-cut. For example, let's imagine a member of your team approaches you for a quick coaching conversation about an important meeting they have later in the day. You can draw on your own experience to ask powerful questions that will cut to the core of what they need, in a timely way. You can raise awareness for the coachee rather than simply sharing what you would do. By using your understanding of the organizational context and incorporating multiple stakeholder perspectives, you can coach them to improve their thinking and deepen their understanding. You've used your expertise as a shortcut to coach your colleague rather than tell them what you would do.

There will be times when the most useful thing you can do is to share a piece of knowledge or expertise. It may be a piece of knowledge they don't have, or something that is holding them back from making further progress on a bigger priority.

Tensions between leading and coaching

Leader coaches are a brilliant asset to any organization, and being one is personally fulfilling. However, it can be challenging because you have leadership responsibility within the organization.

Accountability for results

For a moment let's separate the two roles of leader and coach. A leader has accountability to deliver. A coach in the purist sense does not. It's likely that your performance at work is measured by outcomes and results (the 'what') and the behaviours (the 'how') with which these results are achieved. The pressure for results may push you to use your most ingrained behaviours, such as giving the answer to get the quickest solution. You may also feel strongly about achieving results which could be connected to your identity or maybe a bias for action. This can run very deep for people because in the history of humanity an action bias was vital for survival for our ancestors.

In her book, *Conversational Intelligence*, Judith Glaser invites us to reflect on what we can learn from those times when inherent action bias runs riot over our learnt coaching behaviours.[5] This might be what she calls going into 'Tell-Sell-Yell' mode, where we get progressively more forceful in our approach to get things done, putting ourselves as leaders at the centre, and seeing our own perspective as the most important. We'd suggest that everyone reading this book, and its authors, have been there at one time or another. The key to choosing a different approach is reflecting, learning and being intentional about what you choose to do next time.

Expectations of your team and organization

Further tension may be created from your organizational or team context. Your team might be used to being given the answers, have negative or misinformed perceptions of coaching, or have different expectations of you as a leader. Committing to a coaching approach where you let go of expertise will require strength of character, consistency, agility and strong ongoing communication. Your gift to your team and the organization is to support the development of self-starting, independent individuals who have the confidence to find their own solutions and grow for the long term. Explicitly signalling a change or shift in approach and being open about your own journey as a leader coach can help the team in this situation.

Making a subtle shift in the way that you use your expertise can help your team adapt to a coaching style of leadership. You can intentionally use your expertise and experience to illuminate the inner workings of your organization and how decisions are made. In the article 'Millennial managers can change company culture for the better', the author suggests 'try to share your experiences instead of giving answers when offering learnings to your team. Let them judge if and how your experience might fit into the situation they are trying to solve.'[6]

We noticed this in action recently with a summer internship programme. The temptation when having a younger, less experienced colleague join the team might have been to tell them what to do. What we noticed was quite the opposite. The approach taken by several leader coaches in our organization was to create space for their interns to explore. They were encouraged to network widely, often without the senior colleague present, and were trusted to collaborate and build their own relationships. This meant that they heard different perspectives across the organization, followed their curiosity, and asked questions. They had time to think and consider the bigger picture.

A colleague kindly shared her own experience as an intern:

> From the perspective of a new graduate (completely new to the working world), I definitely experienced a safe space to flourish in my internship. The job itself was very enjoyable, but what I was able to take from it is priceless and will follow me through every step of my career. During my time, there was a perfect amount of teaching and provisions to learn on my own. In my opinion, this is the most beneficial thing you can do for people starting their careers, being responsible for your own success is great practice for all stages of your career.

This programme could have easily been several months of information sharing and low-level tasks, but it became something much more powerful and impactful. New insights were shared, and a diverse range of perspectives were brought to the projects they worked on, creating learning for all.

Your reflections

We've explored different ways you can use your expertise to inform your approach as a leader coach. What insights are you gaining? Use the questions below to prompt further reflection and note down your responses.

- What's it like for you when you are told what to do? What impact does it have on your engagement, development and longer-term performance?
- What do you notice about yourself in the moments when you are tempted to give answers rather than use coaching skills? (For example, feeling under pressure, fear of poor results, sensing pushback from others, noticing expectations of others, etc.)
- What helps you to use your coaching skills rather than give a solution?
- With all of this in mind, how can using and sharing your expertise when you are coaching ever be helpful? How do you know? What helps you decide when to do this?

Using your expertise as a leader coach

Here are some ways that we've seen leader coaches successfully make a shift from giving answers and solutions to coaching:

1 **Lead with a 'pull' style.** As we have explored, just because you have decided to give coaching a prominent place in your leadership style doesn't mean that you must dismiss all the valid expertise, knowledge and experience that you've developed. It is about choice

and considering the needs of others and the organization. A 'push' approach (providing direction, giving guidance, sharing knowledge) remains a valuable part of your toolkit. However, a 'pull' approach (being curious, asking powerful questions, deep listening) will increase the skill and capability that you have as a leader, and likely the results of your team. Build skills in using both, and importantly, consciously choose when to use them so that you become more adaptable to frequently moving along the continuum of 'pushing' and 'pulling'. You can use your knowledge and experience to guide how you use a 'pull' style, for example, to help you ask questions that will have the most impact.

2 **Accept that you'll never have all the answers.** A leader who only passes on their expertise and knowledge creates a conveyor belt of ideas, shaped by their own views and opinions. It can be a narrow and restrictive approach. The most innovative ideas and solutions come from diverse thought and so organizations must leverage all the brilliant expertise and knowledge they have within them. Shifting to become a leader coach is fundamental to achieve this. As you accept that you don't have all the answers, your mind opens and you become curious to understand others' answers and truths. This can have a profound impact on your brain. In the article 'Your brain is hooked on being right', the author suggests 'there's (another) hormone that can feel just as good as adrenaline: oxytocin. It's activated by human connection and it opens up the networks in our executive brain, or prefrontal cortex, further increasing our ability to trust and open ourselves to sharing.'[7] They go on to say that 'Your goal as a leader should be to spur the production of oxytocin in yourself and others, while avoiding (at least in the context of communication) those spikes of cortisol and adrenaline.' Think about what this means for you as a leader coach – the way you communicate and lead can not only grow innovation, but also strengthen trust, openness, engagement and innovation.

3 **Develop independence.** When you let go of emphasizing your own expertise, others will feel that their experience and knowledge is valued. They will feel trusted. It builds their belief in being able to work through a similar solution or challenge in the future. You can

also help others build their own coaching capabilities, creating teams and individuals who can deliver results, and do their best thinking for and among themselves. It's a solid recipe for long-term, sustainable success.

These themes are explored further in Chapter 7, which is about bringing your leader coach approach to team leadership. It will help you explore in more depth how you can apply your coaching skills and mindset to build a strong team.

Final thoughts

In this chapter we have explored the notion of 'letting go of expertise'. Should you? Could you? We have considered the shifting nature of leadership and the role of expertise in your identity as a leader. We explored what is lost and gained by letting go of expertise in this context – for you, for your team and beyond. If you're reading this, you've already embraced a leadership style that is essential in meeting the highly complex challenges and rapidly changing workplace. We invite you to hold your experience lightly, to stay in service of others and step into the discomfort of your shifting identity. So, take a deep breath and embrace the opportunity to coach while letting go of expertise, and all this will open up for you. The next chapter builds on this to explore how you can approach your ongoing development.

References

1 Zenger, J and Folkman, J (2015) How Developing a Coaching Culture Pays Off: Dramatically Improve Your Organization, White Paper, 2 December, https://zengerfolkman.com/wp-content/uploads/2019/05/How-Developing-a-Coaching-Culture-Pays-Off-LRC.pdf/ (archived at https://perma.cc/3J92-7GYF)
2 Willyerd, K (2015) Millennials want to be coached at work, *Harvard Business Review*, 27 February, www.hbr.org/2015/02/millennials-want-to-be-coached-at-work (archived at https://perma.cc/G85W-MTX2)

3 Bungay Stanier, M (2020) *The Advice Trap: Be humble, stay curious and change the way you lead forever*, Box of Crayons Press, Toronto

4 Cox, C and Flynn, S (2022) *Climate Change Coaching: The power of connection to create climate action*, Open University Press, London

5 Glaser, J E (2014) *Conversational Intelligence: How great leaders build trust and get extraordinary results*, Bibliomotion Inc, New York

6 Kralova, U (2021) Millennial managers can change company culture for the better, *Harvard Business Review*, 27 October, www.hbr.org/2021/10/millennial-managers-can-change-company-culture-for-the-better (archived at https://perma.cc/XCJ8-BT2F)

7 Glaser, J E (2013) Your brain is hooked on being right, *Harvard Business Review*, 28 February, www.hbr.org/2013/02/break-your-addiction-to-being (archived at https://perma.cc/LDU4-R3L9)

Developing as a leader coach   3

ANDY MURPHY

You must be the change you wish to see in your life

MAHATMA GANDHI

In order to learn, you've got to want to learn. The same is true of development. Wherever you find yourself in your life and career right now, pause for a moment and reflect on the opportunities, challenges and experiences that have brought you here. Whatever your reflections, it's certain that the narrative and plot twists of your life story so far have served to develop and grow you into the leader coach that you recognize today. Why then should you think about developing your leader coach skills even further?

In this chapter I'll explore some of the key tenets for development as a leader coach by reflecting on key moments in my life and offering questions that you can use for your own reflection.

From father to son: Lessons from my dad

My dad was 15 years old when he left school. He'd grown up in Britain during the Second World War and its aftermath. The new Labour government, elected under a programme of radical change in 1945, promised to wipe out poverty and hardship across society. The reforms ushered in didn't quite extend to the education system, so my dad, thanks to his Irish Catholic heritage, went to a convent school where he was taught by nuns, which was a miserable experience for him and undoubtedly played a part in his desire to get out of the education system as soon as he could. But career options available to men with minimal educational achievements in the late 1950s in Sheffield, South Yorkshire boiled down to a choice of two industries: steel or coal. So coal it was.

He was determined that it wasn't going to end there for him. His engineering job in the coal industry involved 12-hour shifts; mornings, days and nights. This was punishing, hard work with precious little free time. And yet he somehow found the time to go to night school, gain qualifications, and secure promotion to the role of shift charge engineer, all despite having a young family and an arduous job. Where did this energy and desire for progress come from? His response when I asked him this question was 'I needed to better myself.'

While I might have railed against the notion in my youth, I think that parents are responsible for so many of the attitudes and sensibilities that they pass onto their offspring. And while I didn't get to spend a lot of time with my dad as a child, there was always some thinking to be done and lessons to reflect on whenever I did. I remember vividly the winter of 1982, struggling with the choices I needed to make about which subjects I would be taking on to 'O'-Level (a secondary education level qualification that kids in the UK undertook from age 14). While we had fragments of discussions, I was intent on avoiding the subject for as long as possible, until one evening, after a 12-hour day shift (6 am to 6 pm) my dad called me to the dining room table and said, 'Let's talk about your options. Talk me through what you're thinking.' Then he just sat and listened. He didn't tell me what to do; he just sat by me while I tried to work it out for myself. As I recall this, I can feel the awkwardness and frustration of searching for the words to describe what I really thought – I ached just to be told what to do. I came away from that conversation with clarity and a decision, I became sure of myself.

From conversations with coaches over the years, the roads leading to a career in the coaching profession usually start and are shaped by our relationships with those who have had influence over us. As I reflect, I think that this relationship more than any other contributed to my desire to coach others; it's certainly part of the story of who I am, as discussed in Chapter 1. Like my dad, I was motivated by the idea of a better life. For me this involved wanting to work in a place where people challenged my thinking. I also wanted to connect with others – and, very importantly, wear a suit to work.

A few years ago, at my mum and dad's golden wedding anniversary, my young nephew explained to me his thoughts on how he'd like to develop himself in his career. When asked how he'd come to these decisions he replied: 'Grandad had a good chat with me, well I say chat – it was mostly just me talking and him listening.' With that in mind, I'd like to dedicate this chapter to my dad; the very first leader coach in my life.

Development and growth as a leader coach

When you think about it, a development mindset is a prerequisite for the leader coach. Seeking knowledge and personal growth for yourself needs to happen to be able to extend the desire for growth to others. In this context, apart from personal drive or motivation, a development mindset doesn't just mean that you need to have a huge number of books read, courses attended, TED Talks watched, podcasts listened to or qualifications attained. According to Adult Development Theory, activities like these will give you the information, skills and knowledge you need to know to develop (categorized as horizontal development).[1] But that's not the whole story. To help you grow, you also need to consider the concept of vertical development, which is concerned with how the way you think evolves. Three factors are essential, explored here from a self-development perspective, and revisited in Chapter 9 to consider how you can develop others and strengthen your organization.

1 Stretch experiences (sometimes referred to as heat experiences): if you're not uncomfortable in some way, you probably won't be motivated to learn.

2 Colliding perspectives: the opportunity to learn from different perspectives.

3 Elevated sense-making: self-reflection is essential to make meaning of your experience.

Importantly, you need to experience all three of these factors to optimize personal growth, for example:

- Leaving out stretch experiences would leave you with no reason to grow – development becomes an intellectual exercise and little of it gets transferred into the real world.

- Leaving out colliding perspectives means that you don't have other potential ways of looking at things. You're in danger of arriving at the same conclusions as before, which means learning doesn't happen.

- Leaving out elevated sense-making means that you don't make sense of what you've experienced and other points of view you've heard. You limit your opportunity to form new perspectives and ways of doing things.

I'll return to these three factors later in this chapter; for now, reflect further on your development as a leader coach. How would you describe your own development mindset?

My story, part one: It starts with me

You have to do the work on yourself first before developing others.

When I was promoted into my first leadership role in the financial services industry at the age of 23, I can remember thinking 'I've made it now, nothing can stop me.' I also remember the very last question I was asked in my final interview for the job: 'How will you deal with 40-something-year-old employees who've been in their roles for years and think that they know best?' (it was the early 1990s), to which I replied: 'I'll work with them to show that I can make things better.' By 'work' I really meant tell. You can guess the rest – my first few months in the job didn't go well at all.

My direct, abrasive style and resultant disconnection with those I led were the result of what I didn't have at the time – a good enough level of self-awareness. And yet, slowly, over time I began to understand that being able to connect better with myself enabled me to connect better with others, and that both are essential qualities to have as both a leader and a coach.

Bring who you are into being a leader coach

Coach supervisor and author Edna Murdoch states that 'Who you are is how you coach.'[2] This quote blew me away when I first heard it because it brought me to the realization that coaching isn't a mechanical process. Coaching models are devised to provide a structured approach, but if these models are supremely effective then what is the point of human-to-human coaching at all? The same principle could also be applied to leadership. If you look around, you'll see a huge number of books, theories and models about leadership. It makes it impossible to decide which model is best to follow, and even then, the same approach applied by two different people could yield entirely different results. A quote from Carl Jung sums up the conclusion of these thoughts perfectly for me:

> Know all the theories, master all the techniques, but as you touch a human soul be just another human soul.

The key to your development as a leader coach therefore comes from cultivating and maintaining an awareness of your internal state. This helps you navigate the complexities and demands of building and maintaining connection, which is an essential facet of being a leader coach.

I have experienced many highly effective leader coaches who, on promotion or role change, 'forget' their connection with themselves because they assumed the role they had been given. Like the 23-year-old version of me, they experienced a level of disconnection with themselves which created a sense of inauthenticity for those around them.

So, what can be done to combat this disconnection? Emotional intelligence (or EQ) holds the key and is a useful source of reflection. EQ is the ability to notice, identify, understand and manage our own feelings and the emotions of others. Daniel Goleman's work on EQ offers us four competencies to consider; how would you assess yourself in respect of each of the following?[3]

1 Self-awareness: being able to recognize the ways in which your emotions impact your behaviour and how you connect with others.

2 Self-management: being able to take control of your emotions to create balance.

3 Social awareness: being able to understand, or read, social surroundings and the feelings of other people.

4 Relationship management: the ability to communicate and interact effectively with people to create bonds, to elicit the best from them.

Studies show that people who score highly in each of these four competencies demonstrate a higher EQ.[4] They have better emotional stability, mental health and physical well-being, as well as having stronger relationships with others. The great news is, unlike IQ, EQ is a learnable skill, so we can all get better at it. I have found that the following activities help me to develop my own level of emotional intelligence by building a greater awareness of who I am and who I could be in given moments, as well as the choices I could make to connect better with others. Which of these could help you develop as a leader coach?

Ways to develop emotional intelligence as a leader coach

FEELINGS UNHOOK

Take some time to notice your emotions as you experience them, in the moment. Identify them for what they are; for example frustration, happiness, jealousy, joy. If words don't come easily to you, describe them instead, for example 'I have a sinking feeling' or 'I'm fizzing with excitement'.

Although these experiences are completely subjective and personal, naming them helps to 'unhook' them from you. In other words, you 'have' the emotion, rather than you 'are' the emotion. The emotion loosens its power over you, giving you the space to choose how to respond.

The following quote from Viktor Frankl particularly resonates here:

Between stimulus and response there is a space. In that space is our power to choose our response. In our response lies our growth and our freedom.

SELF-ASSESSMENT AND VALIDATION

An honest assessment of your personal strengths and weaknesses can create clarity on how you put your strengths to good use, as well as giving you information on what skills you'd like to develop further.

- Make a list of your personal strengths and potential weaknesses.
- Discuss them with people who can offer you objective feedback on how they see these in action for you. You could ask your boss, your team, your peers or a combination.

Balancing your own potentially harsher critique through seeking input from others will give you valuable external insight.

PRACTISING MINDFULNESS

Like the feelings unhook mentioned earlier, mindfulness builds an ability to detach yourself from the grip of thoughts and feelings by just noticing them instead. This helps you develop the practice of being wholly present in the moment, including awareness of everything around you and inside you (for example your environment, physical sensations, thoughts and feelings).

While there are many practical guides available on this subject alone, for me it involves a habit of taking a pause in-between activities to focus on my breathing, and nothing else, for just one minute before proceeding on to the next activity.

LISTENING WITH TOLERANCE, COMPASSION AND EMPATHY

Developing a curiosity and awareness of others' emotions can help you empathize and give appropriate responses to them and their needs, for example offering reassurance to a colleague who is experiencing a lack of confidence, or taking the time to motivate someone who missed out on a promotion.

Beyond asking how someone is feeling, empathetic leader coaches listen carefully, are approachable and recognize underlying emotions so their colleagues feel acknowledged and understood.

PRACTISING SOCIAL AWARENESS

Take some time to notice your environment and context, socially and organizationally. As human beings we consistently interact with others. As a leader coach there is perhaps an even greater emphasis on the quality of your interactions. Social awareness is essential to recognizing moods, internal states and feelings; from the expressions on people's faces and their body language, as well as what they say and do.

These are some of the practices I've found most useful for leader coaches to continue their development and growth. They help you to connect better with yourself so that you can more deeply and authentically connect with others.

Vertical development factor #1: Stretch experiences

The first aspect of vertical development, as discussed earlier, is stretch, or heat, experiences. These experiences are a big part of anyone's developmental journey, including mine.

My story, part two: Facing the heat

Growth is uncomfortable; you have to embrace the discomfort if you want to expand

JONATHAN MAJORS

As my career progressed, I gained the opportunity to attend a two-month residential course, which was designed to equip me with the skills to become an area leader, including the competencies of observation and feedback. This involved many hours of being videoed while coaching and giving feedback. The process was deeply uncomfortable for me (which of us really likes to see themselves on screen?), yet I still look back on this time as being the most instructive in my career. It taught me that discomfort (in this case, from being observed and then receiving feedback) was essential for development and growth. I also learnt that I needed courage and vulnerability to put myself into the sweet spot for development.

Courage over comfort

Of course, observations and feedback are not the only spaces that provide the potential for learning through discomfort; they exist all around us. Think about the work situations you are experiencing at the moment that feel uncomfortable and reflect on why you might be feeling this way. These areas of discomfort offer clues on where to focus your development.

Heat experiences, or uncomfortable moments, provide us with the opportunity to respond when faced with situations that disrupt and disorient our habitual ways of thinking. This heat, or discomfort, is the key to progress and growth. It's scientific fact that objects need to experience tension to move.[5] So do we. But what constitutes a healthy level of tension – as opposed to a feeling of being overwhelmed, which would be of detriment to development and growth? Or conversely, does a feeling of comfort tell you that you could be pushed a little harder? To reinforce this point, here's a quote from psychiatrist Elisabeth Kübler Ross:

> The most beautiful people we have known are those who have known defeat, known suffering, known struggle, known loss, and have found their way out of the depths. These persons have an appreciation, a sensitivity, and an understanding of life that fills them with compassion, gentleness and a deep loving concern. Beautiful people do not just happen.[6]

The key to unlocking this source of development lies in the environment that we create for ourselves and others around us. This is linked to the development mindset I discussed earlier. The intention to welcome discomfort, rather than turn away from it, can come from purposefully seeking opportunities to develop yourself.

Think back to your reflections on 'who am I?' from Chapter 1. Who is the future you that you would like to become? Gaining clarity about the future you is a good starting point for the formation of a personal contract; between who you are now, and who you will be in the future. A personal contract is a statement that describes and reminds you of who you are now and how you work best in times of conflict, challenge and stress in service of the future you.

Your reflections

Think about your experience of discomfort as part of your personal and professional growth. Use the following questions to deepen your reflections.

- What level of heat or discomfort are you prepared to take to progress towards your future self?
- What will help you find courage in these moments?
- How can you bring more discomfort, or healthy tension, into your experiences to help you to develop and grow?
- What experiences do you need to seek to help you grow and develop?

As a leader coach you are granted a unique opportunity to be a focal point for development; becoming comfortable with discomfort is the key to unlocking the door for development of yourself and others.

Vertical development factor #2: Colliding perspectives – the shared learning space

If I have seen further, it is by standing on the shoulders of giants
ISAAC NEWTON

Looking at the second of the three aspects of vertical development, how can bringing in the thoughts and experiences of others help to broaden your perspective? I used to think that engaging in a coaching intervention with someone was always about helping them to improve their performance. As part of working towards my first coaching accreditation I needed to report on several coaching scenarios. I had to reflect on the interventions I used and the results achieved as proof of what I'd done. One of the people I was working with expressed a wish to work on their performance in their job, which they felt wasn't going as well as they had hoped for. Our initial sessions were always good discussions concluding with a perfectly reasonable set of achievable actions to take away. By session three it became apparent that the actions they were taking weren't working. I can remember feeling stuck over which coaching questions I could now ask, or which approaches I could take, that would help them. There was a moment in that third session when we both just looked at each other, exasperated.

Fortunately, I'd become part of a support network of leader coaches undertaking the same accreditation and we were getting together regularly for meetings. I took along this example for advice and help with what I should do. While presenting the issue I was having, I said 'I don't think that my coachee got anything out of our last session.' After listening and reflecting for a moment one of the group asked me: 'Why do you think that was?' To which I replied rather flippantly 'Because we were unable to come up with any actions that would help them move forward.' There then came a response from someone else in the room, which knocked me off my feet: 'How much of this problem is about you coaching the issue rather than the person?' This question was a 'gotcha' moment for me. In my desire to prove 'progress' with a coachee I was expending a lot of effort on coming up with the perfect question to help the coachee come up with the perfect solution, without taking any time at all to examine what was really going on with the coachee themselves. I would not have arrived at this insight if it hadn't been for the help of others and the access to multiple perspectives that this group provided.

As a leader coach it is important, some would say vital, that you connect with other leader coaches if you are interested in developing your coaching practice. Each of us bring different backgrounds, training, opinions and insights, from which new learning can occur. Creating a supportive network can seem a little daunting, but it's often surprising how many people you know who may already be helping you in this regard, including stakeholders and other leader coaches.

The role of coaching supervision for leader coaches

In addition to a support network, it's also worth considering engaging with coaching supervision, a rapidly expanding facet within the coaching profession. It's perhaps sometimes more helpfully termed as coaching super-vision – separating the words to underline the intent, which is to provide a space for enhanced reflection and insight on coaching practices. As well as engaging with this on an individual basis with a qualified coach supervisor, it can also be experienced on a group basis.

As a leader coach, consider how you could use this approach to meet the needs of your ongoing development. Care needs to be taken to ensure that you engage with a supervision group geared towards your needs as a leader coach, as opposed to someone who solely coaches others, particularly as you're likely to have different needs, for example:

- confidentiality and boundaries
- responsibilities as a leader versus responsibilities as a coach
- business ethics and systems thinking

Coaching supervision for leader coaches can take many forms. It's important that the approach acknowledges that leader coaches may not be engaged in formal coaching and instead are using coaching skills in the flow of their everyday work. Here's one suggestion of a format that does this:

- Session length: 90 minutes.
- Session leader: Experienced coach supervisor.
- Participants: Four leader coaches.
- Format:
  - Introductions and connection building: mindfulness and breathing.
  - Check-in: participants and supervisor share what they need to 'park' for the next 90 minutes to be fully present.
  - Individual reflection: how have you been bringing coaching skills and mindset into your leadership during the previous month? When have you missed an opportunity to do this? Consider from your own perspective (self lens), a focus on relationships (others lens), and a focus on the wider organization (organization lens).
  - Sharing, exploration and peer coaching: each participant has 15–20 minutes to share reflections and be coached by the group. The coach supervisor draws attention to the quality of listening and questions, and the themes emerging.
- Close and check-out: participants share appreciation for the session.

It is often said that the professions of leadership and coaching are lonely ones. If you subscribe to this view with a shrug of the shoulders or inaction, it's bad news from a development perspective because you'll miss out on the experiences, knowledge and points of view that may give you the insight you need to help you move forward.

Your reflections

Reflect on the following questions before reading on:

- How can you connect with others to help you reflect on what you're thinking and doing as a leader coach?
- Who do you already know who you could work with in this way?
- What gaps might exist in your network for this purpose? How will you address this?

Vertical development factor #3: Elevated sense-making – the power of reflective practice

Experience is the teacher of all things

JULIUS CAESAR

The third aspect of vertical development is to make sense of and take meaning from experience. It refers to the process of integrating and making sense of experiences and different perspectives to bring about a more advanced point of view. In other words, through reflection we are seeking to turn what we experience and hear into discernible change, growth or development. This quote from Ludwig Wittgenstein provides the backdrop for the need for reflection perfectly for me:

> The limits of my language mean the limits of my world.

The purpose of reflection is to give language to that which is as yet unsaid. It enables you to expand the limits of your world. Developing a regular reflective practice can be challenging. It's important to give some thought to how you could build time into your schedule to make it a regular habit. Some leader coaches I work with like to block out specific time slots in their schedule for a weekly check-in with themselves; some like to book time at the start and/or end of each day to do this. The key point is to make it regular, protected time for you.

A few years ago, I was working closely with a senior colleague who, despite attempts to provide feedback, frequently took credit for the work of others. They showed favouritism towards other colleagues and withheld praise and recognition from those who they saw as a threat to their own ego. This troubled me greatly as it directly impacted upon me and the people I worked with, and I was feeling stuck over what to do about it.

At the same time as this was happening, I was completing some exercises as part of further study to become a coach supervisor. One of these was to make a list of my personal values and then to place my top ten in rank order. The purpose of this was to provide reflection, clarity and understanding on how my personal values impact my attitude, decisions and behaviour. In other words, to develop a greater level of self-awareness. I placed fairness and integrity at the top of my list without hesitation. Suddenly the scales were lifted from my eyes as I drew a connection to the issue that I was experiencing. What I saw happening was at odds with my value of fairness, and this was drowning out my other values that were important to me. My need for fairness was blinding my need for integrity. This reflection provided the insight to take the actions I needed to restore a sense of balance. I learnt something about myself and adjusted my approach.

Your reflections

Think about how you can develop a regular reflective practice that helps you draw learning and insight from your everyday experience. Use the following questions to think through your approach:

- What time of day/day of the week would work for you?
- Will this be individual reflection, with others, or a mix of both?
- What questions will help you reflect on what's most important to your development as a leader coach at this point in time?
- Who or what will help you hold yourself accountable?

So, what do you do with your protected time when you get there? Borton offers a simple model, which provides a great framework for reflective practice:[7]

Start with a blank piece of paper. Recall an event or experience you'd like to think more deeply about. Write your responses to the questions below:

- **What?** Describe what happened in relation to the event or experience, including what you and others have been doing.
- **So what?** Delve into the meaning of what happened, including why you are seeking to reflect on the situation as well as yours and others' feelings in relation to it.
- **Now what?** Consider what you could do next and the potential consequences of different actions.

This simple framework can help you develop from your everyday experiences as a leader coach.

Final thoughts

I regularly hear the phrases 'I'd like to develop, but I'm not sure where to start' or 'I'm done with development now', yet in my experience the opportunities for development are all around us, every day of our lives.

To develop yourself as a leader coach, consider the following:

- Work on yourself before helping others, by building your levels of emotional intelligence.
- Create heat experiences that make you feel uncomfortable enough to learn.
- Connect with others to gain insight from multiple, different perspectives.
- Build a reflective practice that helps you to make sense of things and grow from your experiences.

I'll leave some of the closing words of this chapter to my dad, who says:

> If you're going to learn, you've got to want to learn, else, what difference are you going to make for yourself or anything?

So thanks Dad, for everything.

References

1 Petrie, N (2018) The How-To of Vertical Leadership Development – Part 2: 30 Experts, 3 Conditions, and 15 Approaches, White Paper, Center for Creative Leadership, https://14226776-c20f-46a2-bcd6-5cefe57153f. filesusr.com/ugd/a8b141_7243e9c83c01457eac15f6cd69073de2.pdf (archived at https://perma.cc/SPY3-FRZP)

2 Murdoch, E and Arnold, J (eds) (2013) *Full Spectrum Supervision: 'Who you are, is how you supervise'*, Panoma Press, St Albans

3 Goleman, D (1995) *Emotional Intelligence: Why it can matter more than IQ*, Bantam Books, Inc, New York

4 Boyatzis, R E and Sala, F (2004) Assessing Emotional Intelligence Competencies, www.eiconsortium.org/pdf/Assessing_Emotional_Intelligence_Competencies.pdf (archived at https://perma.cc/2QHM-UXM6)

5 Study Smarter (2020) Tension, www.studysmarter.co.uk/explanations/physics/dynamics/tension/ (archived at https://perma.cc/278D-ABMJ)

6 Kübler-Ross, E (1975) *Death, the Final Stage of Growth*, Touchstone, New York

7 Borton, T (1970) *Reach, Touch and Teach: Student concerns and process education*, McGraw Hill, New York

PART TWO
Others lens
Being a leader coach with employees and teams

Organization lens:
Having an impact on the
organization

Others lens:
Being a leader coach with
employees and teams

Self lens:
Focusing
on you as a
leader
coach

Leader coach in the employee life cycle

4

NUHA AL MOOSA

We begin Part 2 of this book by looking at bringing a leader coach approach to your everyday leadership. You have a huge opportunity to apply coaching mindset and skills to your role in the employee life cycle, from when an employee joins the organization, to setting goals, managing performance, strengthening engagement, giving feedback, delegating and ongoing development. We'll explore how each of these elements can be implemented using a coaching mindset and skills. Sir John Whitmore, one of the pioneers of coaching in organizations, says that coaching 'unlocks people's potential to maximize their own performance.'[1] There are many tools and frameworks that will help you do this. The ones included are those that I've seen to be most useful for leader coaches to use as part of their role in the employee life cycle. In this chapter we'll cover:

- talent attraction and recruitment
- goal setting
- managing performance and strengthening engagement
- development
- end-of-year/performance reviews

Talent attraction and recruitment

Growing a relationship built on coaching mindset and skills starts from how you approach talent attraction and recruitment. Your first connection with a future team member is likely to be as part of an interview process. During this process, it's important to be aware of your unconscious bias. But what do we mean by that? The American Psychological Association defines unconscious bias, or implicit bias, as 'a negative attitude, of which one is not consciously aware, against a specific social group.'[2] During the attraction and selection process, it's important to be aware of the risk of forming a first impression of candidates, irrelevant of any criteria pertinent to the role advertised. For example, you might be influenced by a candidate's photo, or their home town. This may be due to your personal experience, or comfort with what is familiar to you. If your decision is strongly influenced by your biases, it will result in a less diverse workforce with a smaller range of perspectives and life experiences, leading to limited problem-solving, innovation and strategic planning.[3] It's vital that you recognize and minimize your own unconscious biases across every step of the recruitment process.

To do this, you must first be aware of your biases. Educate yourself by paying attention to your own values and beliefs. Understand the current assumptions you have and where they stem from. Then, acknowledge them. Chapter 1 explored how your values and beliefs shape who you are, and it's worth revisiting this chapter to raise your awareness of how they shape potential biases. One way of doing this work is to request support from your peers to observe you and provide you with feedback. This is a powerful way to role model curiosity, growth mindset and openness to feedback. Other techniques to help combat biases in recruitment are to opt for blind resume/CV screening and utilize technology to hide elements from the resume that may influence your decision. You can also take a deep dive into understanding how bias in the recruitment process may be contributing to any low diversity in your team or organization, for example if there is a low proportion of women in senior positions.

The example below of Ali illustrates how unconscious bias can impact team engagement. (The examples throughout this chapter are inspired by leaders and leader coaches, but some elements have been changed to anonymize the individuals.)

Ali was a highly competitive leader who was looking for a candidate to lead an extremely skilled, technical team. Due to his respect and admiration for his mentor, Ali unconsciously narrowed his candidate shortlist to those individuals that his mentor would approve of, missing out on some key elements required for the role. In less than one month of the new candidate joining the workplace, Ali received complaints from four of the five existing team members about the behaviour and technical gaps of their newly hired team lead. His unconscious bias had led to him recruiting someone who wasn't a good fit for the role.

Talent attraction and selection is merely the beginning of an employee's life cycle, so how do you ensure a smooth integration into the organization? For starters, you will want to show them a warm welcome and maintain the excitement of having them on board. It's important for all team members to get to know their new colleague, understand why they were hired, and grasp the value they will contribute to the overall team.

Goal setting

One of the important things you'll do in the early weeks and months with a new team member is set goals with them. Let's explore how you can take a coaching approach to goal setting, defined by the Cambridge dictionary as: 'the process of deciding what you want to achieve or what you want someone else to achieve over a particular period.' Typically towards the end of the year, as well as when someone joins the team, leaders discuss and agree priorities and goals for the year ahead. As a leader coach, it's important for you to understand your organization's bigger picture, purpose, strategy and priorities for the year ahead so that you can cascade to your team. This is essential for agreeing goals that are strategically aligned and meaningful.

An effective leader coach will begin goal-setting conversations with a review of progress and learning from the previous year. This may have been covered as part of the year-end review conversation.

A leader coach will bring the key points into the goal-setting conversation to build on what was discussed. There are many frameworks that can help you set goals, and three are included here: GROW, SMART and STAR.

GROW: A framework for goal setting

The GROW framework is a simple and powerful framework that can guide you as a leader coach any time you need to set goals or agree a course of action. It is explained briefly below and covered in more detail in Chapter 7 on leading teams.

- Goal: What do you want to achieve by the end of this meeting/month/year?
- Reality: What is happening now? Where are you in relation to the goal?
- Options: What ideas can you think of to achieve the goal? (Generate as many options as possible to help broaden thinking rather than stopping after the most obvious ones.)
- Will: What will you commit to, who else will help you, what are your milestones?

SMART goals

The SMART goals framework is a useful way to test a goal and make it rigorous. Once you have agreed a goal, challenge your thinking about it by asking the following questions and making any changes to make the goal more robust:

- Specific/Simple: Is it specific and simple? Will it help you achieve your overall goal/strategy?
- Measurable/Meaningful: Is it measurable? Can you monitor progress against the goal? Is it meaningful to you, the team, the organization?

- Achievable/Aligned: Is it achievable within the time frame and the resources available? Is it in alignment with the overall strategy? With your skills and capability? With what interests you?

- Realistic/Responsible: Is it challenging while still practical? Does it impact others/other goals? Is it in conflict with other goals?

- Time-framed/Towards: Does it have a clear time frame? Will it create progress towards something?

STAR: Reinforcing goal setting

Once goals have been agreed, the STAR framework is useful to reinforce goals and encourage progress in informal conversations:

- Set a Target: using frameworks such as GROW and SMART.
- Achieve: provide ongoing coaching and support on progress and achievements.
- Recognize: celebrate when goals have been achieved, or when milestones have been met.

To further motivate individuals within your team to achieve goals, think about how you build in autonomy, mastery and purpose. Thought leader and author Dan Pink's research into motivation in his book *Drive* shows that these three components are essential to tap into intrinsic motivation:[4]

1 Autonomy: the need to direct your own life and work. What autonomy can be built into how someone achieves a goal?

2 Mastery: the desire to improve and become skilful at something. How can progression towards a goal help someone develop a skill or expertise that is important to them? Someone who seeks mastery needs to attain it for its own sake.

3 Purpose: investing in the bigger picture by connecting personal goals to organizational targets. How does the goal link and align with organizational strategy and purpose, as well as what's important to the individual?

The example that follows is an illustration of how a leader could put this into practice with their team:

At the start of the year Zainab held a workshop with her team to cascade the corporate goals for the year ahead. The organization she works for was transitioning from being oil and gas dependent towards becoming more environmentally and economically sustainable. She needed to make sure that this shift in strategy and the related annual goals were clear to all team members. She worked with individuals to agree and align on the outcomes they needed to achieve, and the most effective and efficient way to deliver them. Personally, she understood why the company was transitioning and believed in the bigger picture, and wanted her team to understand this for themselves. She considered simply cascading the goals but knew that she would generate greater engagement if her team members did this thinking for themselves.

In the workshop, she communicated the agenda, set the scene, and then asked her team members:

- What is the company's purpose?
- What is its strategy to get there?
- How can we contribute to its success?
- What do we need to start doing?
- How do we do it?
- What should we continue doing?
- What should we do differently?

Her aim was to ensure everyone was on the same page, clarify areas of concern and address individual challenges. Her team members left the workshop having greater clarity on the rationale behind the goals and how their roles contributed.

Managing performance and strengthening engagement

Once goals have been agreed it's important to continually review progress and strengthen engagement, spotting opportunities for learning and coaching along the way. This is where your leader coach perspective and skills can accelerate your impact. Every interaction you have with someone for whom you have managerial responsibility is an opportunity to increase engagement, enhance performance, and strengthen belonging. One of the greatest tools in your toolkit to do this is the regular check-in.

Regular check-ins

Regular weekly or monthly check-ins are important for you to engage individually with team members, review progress and navigate challenges. A simple structure for you to use as a leader coach is to ask your team members three questions:

- What's going well? This gives an opportunity to celebrate success and reinforce learning.
- Where are you stuck? Spotting challenges early on will help to problem solve and coach your team member to develop their problem-solving skills.
- How can I help? Showing your support helps team members learn how to leverage your skills and experience and develops trust and psychological safety.

By regularly using this structure your team members will expect each check-in to be a useful conversation, as shown in the example. This approach supports their performance and progress, and shows that you care about them as an individual.

> During his individual check-in conversations Qasim strengthened belonging and psychological safety by encouraging dialogue, asking questions instead of providing solutions and actively listening to his team members. He made sure he spoke last, so as not to influence someone else's thought process. As a leader coach, he urged his team members to speak up and challenge the status quo respectfully.

Plan-Do-Check-Act (PDCA)

One of the tools you can use in your regular check-ins to track progress with individuals, or a team, is Plan-Do-Check-Act (PDCA). This is a method you can integrate with a coaching approach by asking open questions to enhance the quality of thinking and capability of your team.

- Are we on track?
- What got in the way?
- How could we tackle this situation?
- What could we do differently?
- How can I support?

PDCA is a useful tool to proactively review performance informally prior to a more formal review, which may happen at mid-year as well as the end of the year. By checking in on employees' emotions as well as performance, you are demonstrating care towards their well-being and strengthening a sense of purpose and passion.

Choosing what approach to take – situational leadership

There are situations where an approach other than coaching is needed. For example, if an employee is doing something for the first time, or doesn't have the capability or knowledge to achieve a goal, you may need to give direction and guidance rather than coaching. Alternatively, consider a situation where an employee is highly skilled but isn't performing at the level you'd expect. A directive style is unlikely to be effective, instead you'll need to understand what is getting in the way. A framework that can help you determine what approach to take with different team members is situational leadership, originally created by thought leaders in management and organizational behaviour Paul Hersey and Ken Blanchard.[5] It prompts you to think about your employees in terms of their ability and motivation. It proposes that you need to adapt your approach with each person based on their level of ability and motivation in each situation. You need to be able to direct, coach, participate or delegate depending on the situation. It has a short-term and long-term focus and is especially useful when performance or progress has stalled, or when you are leading a new employee.

1 **Telling, directing or guiding.** Use when an employee has low levels of ability or experience in what they are working on, as well as low motivation or confidence. You give clear direction and guidance on how to proceed. In the short term, this approach creates momentum. It's more directive than a typical coaching approach; however, it is still sometimes needed. Use it sparingly; if you find yourself needing to frequently direct someone over a long period of time, it could be a sign of poor performance or poor fit for the role.

2 **Selling, coaching or explaining.** Use when an employee has low levels of ability or experience in what they are working on but is highly motivated to learn. You give clear direction and recognize the enthusiasm and commitment of the employee, giving plenty of opportunities for discussion and development.

3 **Participating, coaching or facilitating.** Use when an employee has a high level of ability but isn't making progress due to a low level of motivation or confidence. You explore what the barriers are to performance and coach any areas of stuck-ness. This is a follower-driven approach. If you become 'stuck' with needing to use this approach with someone over a longer time period, consider why this is. You may need to take a different approach.

4 **Delegating, empowering or motivating.** Use when an employee has a high level of ability and is motivated and confident in what they are doing. You build on what the person is learning through open questions and help them identify improvements.

The situational leadership framework helps you to adapt your approach to the individual and situation, rather than assuming a coaching approach will work all the time. It is useful for determining your approach in the short term, and a valuable framework to have in your toolkit, especially to help you examine the fit between your leadership style and an employee's level of skill and motivation in a specific situation.

Feedback

It's important to maintain ongoing dialogue between you and your employees, and to give frequent feedback on both their performance and behaviour in a structured and timely manner. This reinforces success and encourages employees to build on what's working well. Constructive feedback is essential so that team members know when they need to change their approach and understand the impact they are having on others or their progress towards their goals. Sometimes it's tempting to hold back from giving constructive feedback through a fear of damaging a relationship, or a discomfort with any potential disagreement or conflict. If this resonates with you, go back to Chapter 1 to reflect on what it is within you that is holding you back. You're doing the individual and the team a disservice when you hold back useful information about their performance, behaviour or impact.

The great news is that by using your leader coach skills in all aspects of your leadership you are creating the conditions for honest, transparent and future-focused conversations. This makes it easier to give and receive feedback, and give the tougher messages in a way that shows you care about the people who work for you. The SEED model is a structure that can help you frame feedback, and can be useful to plan how to give constructive feedback as well as feedback and appreciation about great work:

- Set the scene: bring the conversation back to the incident or behaviour that happened.

- Explain your understanding: be simple and factual in your explanation of what you observed.

- Explore other perspectives: offer the employee an opportunity to tell you their side of the story, and seek evidence.

- Determine the next steps: discuss the way forward.

The key is to focus on the event or behaviour to enhance performance and develop individual team members.

Understanding individual differences

Walking in the shoes of your team members is important because it helps you understand what they need from you to perform at their best. The most powerful thing you can do is to listen intently and pay attention – to what they say, don't say, body language, facial expression and tone of voice, as well as the words they use. Each of us is shaped by our own unique life experiences, which have formed our underlying beliefs and identity (see Chapters 1 and 2 for a deep exploration of what shapes us). As a leader coach there are many frameworks that can help you understand individual differences, such as the Myers–Briggs Type Indicator (MBTI), which is based on Carl Jung's theories of personality development and the role of the unconscious.[6,7] The MBTI defines eight preferences; how we are energized (introversion and extraversion), how we process information (sensing and intuition), how we make decisions (thinking and feeling), and how we interact with the world around us (perceiving and judging).

The example shows how a leader coach could use their knowledge of individual differences using the MBTI framework.

Throughout the year, and particularly during performance reviews, Khalid reflected on the personalities of his team members and how they were different/similar to him. He knew that he had a preference for extraversion and got his energy from engaging with others; however, he was also aware that one of his team members was more introverted and got their energy from reflecting and time working alone. While he was talking through ideas with them, he made sure he provided them with the space to allow more thinking time. When he discussed the bigger picture with another team member, he understood that they had a preference for sensing and so preferred to start by understanding the details to build up to the big picture perspective. This was different from Khalid, who had a preference for intuition and was very comfortable starting with the big picture and playing with ideas and possibilities. His knowledge of the individual differences among his team meant that he could adapt his approach with each person to get the best from them. Without this awareness Khalid would likely have approached everyone in the same way. He would have missed opportunities to develop, engage and strengthen performance.

There are many frameworks that can help you as a leader coach to appreciate individual differences. The MBTI is just one example. Whichever you use, make sure that you use it as a source of insight to help build deeper understanding of your team, and awareness and appreciation of difference. Tools like this can also build transparency and trust with your team, especially when you also openly share your profile with them.

Leader reflection – be curious, not judgemental

When people don't behave or perform in line with expectations it can be very easy to jump to conclusions. Your capacity to remain curious about what's going on for someone else will help get to underlying root causes and find a way forward. Perceptual positions is a tool that encourages you to challenge and broaden your perspective about what's causing someone to behave differently than expected. It's a structured methodology for you to take at least three different perspectives: your own perspective, someone else's, and an objective observer. We'll explore it in more detail in Chapter 6 about shifting stuck thinking and behaviour; for now here's an example of it being used by a leader coach, Mariam.

Mariam reflected on when one of her team members, Ahmed, did not report to work nor notify her of his absence. When Mariam reached out, Ahmed simply said that he'd be coming in the following day. Mariam was disappointed with this response, and noticed she was starting to get upset and create her own story about what was happening. She took a few minutes to use the perceptual positions framework to suspend judgement and consider their next steps.

- In the first perspective, through Mariam's eyes, Ahmed behaved carelessly and irresponsibly. She noticed she felt disappointed and disrespected.

- She then shifted to the second perspective, to consider Ahmed's point of view. She considered as many reasons as she could think of that might have caused him to act in the way he did; he could have been sick, his child may have been unwell, there may have been a bereavement, maybe he was about to call Mariam, perhaps he was waiting for an in-person conversation rather than a phone call, maybe he was worried about something at work, there could be conflict with a colleague, or even with Mariam. Mariam noticed that as she suspended judgement and became curious her frustration towards Ahmed subsided. She knew this was not typical of Ahmed's behaviour.

- Finally, she shifted to the third perspective – that of an objective observer. If she was a fly on the wall looking at this situation, what could be going on and what should she do next? The objective observer position offered a different perspective, encouraging Mariam to hear Ahmed out before deciding what to do next, that Ahmed likely had a good reason for his behaviour, and that Mariam could coach him if needed.

Once in the office, Mariam arranged to speak to Ahmed in-person, privately. She listened to what he had to say and learnt that Ahmed had been feeling overwhelmed during the last few weeks at work and the stress of a family illness had pushed him to a point where he felt he couldn't talk about it. Mariam worked with him to rearrange some of his work responsibilities and timelines for the coming weeks, and used this as an opportunity to agree how they could communicate and work together in future if a similar situation arose. It became an opportunity for Mariam to build rapport and empathy, enabling Ahmed to openly share his challenge, which led to a fruitful discussion, coaching opportunity and mutual agreement on the way forward.

Managing underperformance

There will be occasions when the quality of your employee's work is below the required level, or their behaviour is unacceptable. It's important to address this in a timely and respectful way to ensure business sustainability and to minimize negative impact on the wider team. As a leader coach this is an opportunity to first practise performance-focused coaching, and to use some of the tools from this chapter, such as situational leadership and the SEED feedback model. If performance or behavioural issues continue, it's likely that these approaches won't be enough. It's important to recognize that you are now dealing with underperformance. You need to respond to this so that you are putting the team and business needs first, ahead of the underperforming individual. This can be the most challenging part of any leader coach's role. When handled with respect, compassion and a focus on what needs to be different, it can be a significant point in your relationship with an employee. It can mean the beginning of a turnaround in performance, or sometimes is the first step towards them finding another role or organization that is a better fit. It's likely that your organization has a process in place, such as creating a performance improvement plan with the individual, with measurable milestones for an improvement in performance or behaviour.

You can still bring your leader coach mindset and skill to these conversations. Strike a balance between understanding the reasons behind underperformance, and reiterating performance and behaviour expectations, along with the consequences of these not being achieved. Ask open questions and be curious about what is going on for the individual. Depending on the steps in your organization's process for managing underperformance, you're likely to need to develop an action plan to get performance back on track. You can use goal-setting approaches outlined in this chapter, and if appropriate can enable the person to participate in this. It can be a very challenging time for you, the individual and the wider team. Being respectful and clear about what is needed signals your integrity and focus to everyone involved.

Development

Let's shift to one of the most rewarding aspects of taking a leader coach approach: watching your team grow and develop. Seeing others stretch themselves to take on new challenges and build greater confidence and capability, and knowing that you had a part to play in their success, can feel very satisfying. Setting goals for development should be part of your goal-setting approach, alongside setting performance goals. Draw on your organization's approach to employee development to inform your conversations, for example, there may be a competency framework, attributes or skills that the organization has defined as important. You can frame your development conversation around this. Once you have agreed development goals, using the goal-setting frameworks suggested earlier in this chapter, you can coach your team members to plan the steps they will take towards their goals. Two more frameworks that can help development conversations are the 70/20/10 framework and wheel of life tool.[8]

70/20/10 framework

The 70/20/10 framework explores how people learn, grow and change over the course of their careers. It proposes that 70 per cent of learning comes from on-the-job experiences, 20 per cent from learning from others (such as working with a more experienced colleague, a buddy, coach or mentor), and 10 per cent comes from formal training material or courses.

- To leverage the 70 per cent – provide your team members with challenging assignments that stretch them outside of their comfort zones to maximize their potential and maintain motivation. This should be where most learning occurs. It's also where you have a big role to play, by helping to surface learning from on-the-job experience.

- To leverage the 20 per cent – consider colleagues who your team members can learn from, for example those who are more skilled or experienced. Coaching, mentoring and action learning are also included in this category. As a leader coach you can support learning in the 20 per cent in your regular check-ins by asking team members what they are learning, where they are stuck and how they might apply their learning in the future. This is important to help them make meaning of their experience. (In Chapters 3 and 9 we explore how stretch experiences, being exposed to different perspectives and making meaning from experience are three essential ingredients for what's known as vertical (transformational) development.)[9]

- To leverage the 10 per cent – explore when more formal learning is required, keeping in mind that only 10 per cent of learning should come from formal courses and programmes.

This is a useful framework to share with your team members to help them identify opportunities for learning, and to reinforce that there are opportunities for learning in daily experiences. It's also a great way for you to reflect on your ongoing development, as explored further in Chapter 3.

Figure 4.1   Wheel of life

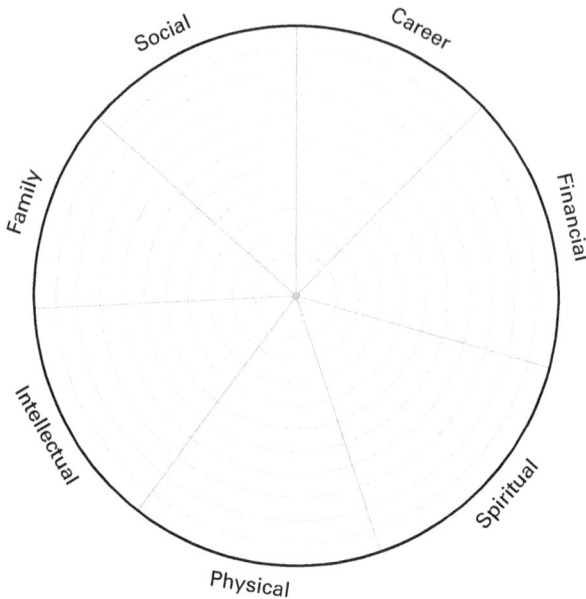

Wheel of life

The wheel of life is a useful and simple tool that broadens a development discussion beyond work to consider the whole person – also known as holistic development. It helps someone to identify how satisfied they are with different aspects of their life, including their career and development. Once they have completed the wheel, they can use this to help set goals that will bring greater balance to what's most important in their life.

How to use the wheel of life:

1 Write a list of all the important aspects in your life. Some examples are shown in Figure 4.1. Your list will be unique to you, and you can have as many as you like. I've worked with some people who have over 15 areas on their wheel of life.

2 Draw a wheel and divide it into segments, one segment for each aspect. Label the segments on the blank wheel, one aspect of your life per segment.

3 Think about each aspect and assign a score to it based on how satisfied you are currently with this aspect of your life. Use a 1–10 scale, with 1 being completely unsatisfied and 10 being totally satisfied.

4 The middle of the wheel equates to a score of 1, the outermost rim of the wheel equates to a score of 10. Colour or shade the segment up to the level of satisfaction that you identified in the previous step.

5 Repeat the previous step for all the segments.

6 Once all the segments of the wheel are shaded in line with your scores, look at the shape of your wheel. It's likely that your wheel is a bit bumpy – that's typical for most of us. Identify which aspects of your wheel you want to focus on. What goals can you set that will give you a smoother wheel? How can the development opportunities you have in your work help to even out your wheel?

As with the 70/20/10 framework, the wheel of life is a useful tool for you to use to reflect on your ongoing growth as a leader coach in the context of your whole life. I recommend completing it for yourself before using it with team members. It's an excellent way to broaden a development discussion and to help your team members see the interconnections between satisfaction derived from work and home.

End-of-year review

At the end of the year, and sometimes at mid-year, you are likely to be required to conduct a performance review. Become familiar with your organization's approach to assessing performance, in particular paying attention to any rating scales that are used so that you can apply this to each of your team. A performance review is an opportunity to review goals, as well as capture learning, celebrate success and identify areas for development. As a leader coach this is an important moment for engagement and development, as well as reviewing performance. The example shows how Sam, a leader coach, approached it.

Sam made the time to meet with his team to review last year's results against the previously set targets. He called for an 'active' reflection where he recognized each person for their positive performance and probed to recall some of the significant challenges that they had come across. As a leader coach, he was inclusive in his approach, providing positive reinforcement of a job well done, as well as identifying where each person could improve their performance in the year ahead. He asked questions like:

- What did you do well last year?
- What should you continue doing?
- What should you stop or start doing to be even more effective in future?

He invested significant effort in reflecting, with the intent to learn from experience, seek different views, and work towards a brighter, more improved future. In addition, he asked his team to seek 360-degree feedback from those who had worked closely with them. This helped him to gain a comprehensive overview of their capabilities, areas for development and impact on others. This gave team members Sam's honest, constructive and timely feedback, based on personal observation and on-the-job demonstration, as well as feedback from a collective lens. Sam didn't shy away from difficult conversations; he recognized the individual for their achievements as well as what hadn't gone as well. This in turn had an impact on his team members' end-of-year rating and potential progression.

Sam also requested feedback from his team on his own performance and behaviour. He asked:

- What did I do well last year?
- What should I continue doing?
- What should I stop or start doing?

By doing this he role modelled a growth mindset and openness to feedback.

If you have been having regular check-ins and have been transparent about performance, progress and feedback throughout the year, there shouldn't be any new information to be shared at an end-of-year performance review. It should simply be a summary of all the conversations you've had during the year. There shouldn't be any surprises for your team members, or any feedback that hasn't already been shared. When done well, the end-of-year review leads seamlessly into setting goals for the year ahead, as explored at the beginning of this chapter.

Final thoughts

In this chapter I've shared many frameworks, approaches and tools that can help you bring a leader coach mindset and skills into your role as a leader within your organization. I've chosen those that I've seen have the greatest impact in the hands of leader coaches. We've broadly followed the employee life cycle to help you see that there are many opportunities to bring a coaching mindset into how you approach your role, be it when you are attracting or selecting talent, setting goals, developing employees or engaging in regular check-ins with individual team members. Every conversation you have is an opportunity to enhance performance and bring out the best in those around you. In Chapter 5 we'll focus on how you have these conversations – how the words you use impact team members and colleagues. In Chapter 6 we'll look at what you can do when performance or thinking in your team has stalled and you're not making the progress you expected. Chapter 7 then completes this part of the book by taking a team leadership perspective.

References

1 Whitmore, J (2017) *Coaching for Performance: The principles and practice of coaching and leadership*, 5th edn, Nicholas Brealey Publishing, London

2 American Psychological Association (nd) Implicit bias, www.apa.org/topics/implicit-bias (archived at https://perma.cc/UX5M-N7RX)

3 Carnahan, B and Moore, C (2023) Actively addressing unconscious bias in recruiting, *Harvard Business Review*, 16 June, www.hbs.edu/recruiting/insights-and-advice/blog/post/actively-addressing-unconscious-bias-in-recruiting (archived at https://perma.cc/46AT-PL4C)

4 Pink, D (2011) *Drive: The surprising truth about what motivates us*, Riverhead Books, New York

5 Hersey, P and Blanchard, K H (2000) *Management of Organizational Behaviour: Leading human resources*, 8th edn, Pearson, Upper Saddle River, NJ

6 Myers, I B and Myers, P B (1995) *Gifts Differing: Understanding personality type*, CPP, Mountain View, CA

7 Jung, C (2003) *Psychology of the Unconscious*, Dover Publications, Mineola, NY

8 McCauley, C (2022) The 70-20-10 rule for leadership development, Center for Creative Leadership, 24 April, www.ccl.org/articles/leading-effectively-articles/70-20-10-rule/ (archived at https://perma.cc/3VHA-B9AU)

9 Petrie, N (2018) The How-To of Vertical Leadership Development – Part 2: 30 Experts, 3 Conditions, and 15 Approaches, White Paper, Center for Creative Leadership, https://14226776-c20f-46a2-bcd6-5cefe57153f.filesusr.com/ugd/a8b141_7243e9c83c01457eac15f6cd69073de2.pdf (archived at https://perma.cc/SPY3-FRZP)

Words make worlds – the power of language

5

TONY WORGAN

Language has a profound impact on your working relationships, your effectiveness as a leader coach and even your well-being. You can only learn others' thoughts, feelings and perspective through their behaviour and what they say. Language is our means to convey our world to others and to understand their world. When you appreciate how words make worlds, then you become a more effective leader coach.

I met Raj for lunch. As usual, he said he was exasperated with a team member. He said, after numerous performance feedback conversations, there was still no improvement. Raj felt stressed by the lack of change and attributed the blame for the unproductive conversations to his team member.

Raising his voice, Raj said, 'He just doesn't get it. *Every* conversation is the same. He *never* listens. He's stuck on the beach and the tide has gone out.' I confess I thought they were both stuck on the beach together and I was there with them!

I'm sure you've experienced stuck conversations. You may recognize the impulse to blame. Did you notice Raj's exaggerated, grandiose language? Was every conversation the same? Does his colleague 'never' listen? What did Raj mean when he said 'He just doesn't get it'?

Were his feelings leaking out in the language he used with his team member? Raj's intention was, ostensibly, to offer feedback to improve performance.

I asked Raj what he wanted his team member to do differently. 'Well, he just needs more "fizz".'

I asked what he meant by 'more fizz'. 'Come on Tony, more fizz; you know…', he said, getting louder, 'MORE FIZZ!'

I wonder, how did Raj's team member make sense of 'more fizz'. What did Raj really want to say and what remained unsaid? It reminded me of a friend who said to me, 'I can't stop, I'm meeting my boss for another guess what's in his head conversation!' I think Raj and his team member were both guessing each other's thoughts. So was I!

In this chapter I'll share some of my experience and learning about the role of language for leader coaches. This knowledge may be necessary but is not sufficient alone to co-create productive conversations. The language you use is entangled with all the other themes explored in this book. This chapter explores language to help you shift attitudes and form useful habits. Chapter 6 will shift focus to the similar and related theme of stuck patterns of behaviour. Together these two chapters will help you find the words and behaviour to step out of unproductive conversations into flourishing working relationships.

Throughout this chapter I'll share examples inspired by leader coaches, like the example of Raj. Some aspects have been changed or stories adapted to anonymize the individuals involved.

Language in the games people play

Think about a workplace conversation that left you and a colleague feeling uncomfortable, confused or agitated. It seemed you each played a role, and at some point, someone switched roles. You wonder, 'what happened there?' The psychologist Eric Berne called this behaviour a game.[1] These repetitive interactions begin with generalized, negative language, often laden with assumption. The language exaggerates or minimizes an aspect of reality. Developing his theory through observation, Berne used concise descriptions of game patterns.

A common game I notice in the workplace he called 'Why don't you – Yes, but...' Leaders who like to have the answers may get caught in this game. Eager to offer advice from a desire to help others, they get stuck in the game, which can shift into another called 'I was only trying to help...'

For example, mine and Raj's conversation about the issue he has with his colleague:

Raj: I can't get Sam to show more fizz in his work. He just never listens.

Me: Why don't you tell him how you feel?

Raj: Yes, but if I do that he'll fly off the handle... nobody likes being told they're rubbish, do they?

Me: Could you ask someone else to have a word?

Raj: Yes, but it's my job to deal with it. I must do it. I am the boss, you know?

Me: How about moving him to another role?

Raj: Yes, but I can't just give in to him, can I? A lot of use you are, mate!

Me: OK, OK, I'm only trying to help.

Raj: Well, don't bother. It's hopeless.

In this example, I'm hooked into a game. I offered help when none was asked for and my responses reinforced the pattern. As a leader coach, you can use your experience to notice what's happening and respond differently from how I did. You may also discover recurring games that reflect your workplace culture. With awareness and courage, you can decline the invitation to take part by changing your words.

Psychologist John James devised a framework called The Game Plan to untangle the knot.[2] The framework offers a series of questions to ask yourself when you notice you are caught up in a game. Here's how it works, continuing the example of my conversation with Raj.

1 What keeps happening between us, repeatedly?
When I see Raj he complains to me about his team members.

2 How does it start?
Raj moans about someone's failings.

3 What happens next?
I offer a suggestion.

4 And then?
Raj rejects my help or suggestion, and I feel frustrated.

5 How does it end?
I run out of suggestions and Raj sounds annoyed. I wish I hadn't got involved.

6 How do I feel at the end?
Uncomfortable, exasperated, bored with hearing him moan.

7 How do I think the other person feels at the end?
Raj gets annoyed with me, annoyed with his team, stuck.

When you have answered the questions, there is an *extra mystery question*, which may be revealing:

8 What secret messages do you think you are sending each other?
Me: Stop moaning to me and do something!
Raj: I want some help, but I don't know how to ask for it.

The answers to question eight are informative and say something about what's really going on. I don't like moaning and stopped listening. Raj is stuck and feels vulnerable. When you begin to make sense of the repeated behaviour, options emerge to choose a more usefully worded response. For example:

Raj: I can't get Sam to show more fizz in his work. He just doesn't listen.

Me: That sounds difficult for you. I won't discuss it with you now. I have an appointment.

Or:

Raj: I can't get Sam to show more fizz in his work. He just doesn't listen.

Me: What do you need from me right now?

As a leader coach, when you attend to language, you open the opportunity to find out what's really going on and avoid colluding or starting games. In the rest of this chapter, I want to offer you ways to avoid games and encourage more productive relationships through your use of language. To do this it's useful to create a more transparent structure for your working conversations. Here are some tips I've tried that helped me.

Saying hello – contact and contract

Two useful themes to think about in your reflection are contact and contract with others. In Chapter 8, there's more on contracting in formal coaching relationships. Here we explore everyday interactions in which you express and enquire into why, what and how the team works on tasks and in your relationships. The latter usually gets missed!

Contact – be present, not perfect

As a leader coach when you come together with colleagues you aim to be fully present in the moment, undistracted and aware, accepting yourself and others to enhance the quality of your relationships. You create authentic rapport and when it's broken, you name what's happening and find a way back into rapport again. The German psychiatrist and psychotherapist Fritz Perls called this 'contact'.[3] Being in contact accepts vulnerability, offers transparency and builds trust. If words make worlds, then awareness of language, in the moment, means you are seen by others and see them for who they are. Table 5.1 identifies ways to strengthen contact with others.

Contracting

In my experience, most teams and individuals invest a lot of energy talking about tasks, roles, procedures, etc, and comparatively little time attending to how to work together – noticing the patterns of language and behaviour in your working relationships. It takes courage

Table 5.1   What to be aware of to strengthen contact with others

Preparation It's useful to reflect on what thoughts and feelings you're carrying into a conversation. What dominates? What's relevant to this conversation, here and now? Are you predicting the path and outcome of the conversation? What assumptions and fantasies are there for you? What are your feelings, for example fear, anger, frustration, pressure, etc? Acknowledge to yourself the answers to these questions, to be responsive and present in the moment.
Beginning When you meet people, language and behaviour patterns recur, influenced by culture, ranging from typical social exchanges to the culture of your organization. When we meet, we try to figure what's going on. What's it like for me to be with you, or in this group? Who are you and what will happen between us? Will I come to harm around you? As the psychologist Eric Berne enquired, how do you say 'hello' to someone else? When you meet a stranger, there's often ritual communication, 'Hi, my name's Tony, nice to meet you', followed by a culturally appropriate response. With colleagues you may fulfil social expectations and ask, 'How are you?' Do you really want to know the answer, and do you wait to hear it? You may receive a perfunctory, ritual reply, 'Oh, I'm fine, thanks', which may not be true. So, where you place the emphasis in the question shows your willingness to be present and listen. When you ask 'How are you?' with sincerity, you are present, curious and open to the response.
What comes next? After the language and behaviour of ritual, you may pass time together. These times also often follow a familiar pattern, like the light conversation at social gatherings. You exchange information and experience. You may talk about the weather, sport, appearance, families, etc. As a leader coach you notice what's said, how it's said and what goes unsaid. You look out for choice of words and patterns, some of which are discussed in this chapter. You're careful not to linger too long at these times, as this could avoid moving on to contracting and the agenda.

to talk about working relationships, to notice and name what exists in team dynamics. Some leaders fear this will kick the hornet's nest. So, it's not surprising that it's often left for annual appraisals and away days, or never addressed. What's more effective is to make it an ongoing process to surface how you're working together. This helps to address and solve problems and deliver sustainable change. Questions like those below are a useful starting point for surfacing and exploring how to better work and relate together:

- What needs to be said for us to thrive in our work?
- How can we resolve differences better?

- How can we ensure everyone is included?
- What's your understanding of our purpose; this task, etc?
- How shall we deal with conflict when it arises?
- How can we recover when relationships break down?
- How might we be disappointed in this work?
- What are we avoiding?
- What's happening in the group that's getting in our way?
- How effectively are we working together?
- How is our culture working for you?

Continue this process and you'll create a sense of inclusion and safety in your working relationships. You'll create clarity for the tasks and behaviour you expect. You'll make the boundaries clear – what's OK and not OK around here. This is the language of 'naming' what often goes unsaid, overcoming what Peter Senge called the 'undiscussable' barriers to learning and thriving.[4]

We've covered some of the language of contact and contract. Doing this means you are attuning to yourself and others and enquiring and naming what needs to be named. This is your scaffolding as a leader coach. You promote effective, flourishing working relationships and end any repeated cycles of misunderstanding and misinterpretation. This transparency is key and sets the foundation for what we're exploring next; creating a more open and honest culture through the words you use.

Three rules of openness

Psychologist Steve Karpman offers a simple framework to encourage open communication, originally used for family therapy and very valuable in organizations.[5] Each step requires your skill and care to manage safely and successfully. He surmises that:

Bring It Up, Talk It Up, Wrap It Up.

is better than:

Save It Up, Blow It Up, Mop It Up.

Here's an example to bring this to life, one that may be familiar: you notice that recently your deputy is often late for work. He's become passive and barely contributes to meetings. You've been concerned for some time. You become increasingly annoyed. You waited so long to 'bring it up', now you hope your facial expressions and 'tutting' will induce them to read your mind and say what's going on. You held back, fearing you may 'blow it up', shout, lose your temper and say or do something regrettable. You overhear other colleagues whisper about the behaviour. They wonder what you will do about it. He is an influential person, so they don't 'bring it up' either because they fear retaliation.

Your challenge is to find the language to 'bring it up, talk it up and wrap it up'. In this case it may pay to 'think it up' first and reflect on how to address the issue. You want to make contact, contract and avoid games, to be direct, reasonable and open, to discover what's going on for your deputy without blame. You need language leading through to 'wrap it up' with a sustainable, productive outcome.

A useful approach is to begin with noticing – naming what you experience, 'I've noticed recently you've arrived late several times. I need you to be here on time, so I wonder why this is happening.' As a leader coach, you aim to remain in contact with him. You name with brevity what you've noticed and remain open to what may emerge. You are fully present in the moment so that you respond appropriately to whatever he shares. It's OK for you to share your feelings too. It's perfectly reasonable to express the impact of others on you, whether it's anger, sadness, fear or joy.

Different strokes for different folks

When you greet a colleague, 'Morning, Hussein, what beautiful weather it is today', and he smiles, and replies, 'Morning, yes, it is. Shall we have our coffee break outside today?', you are exchanging what psychologist Eric Berne called strokes.[6] You can think of a stroke as a unit of recognition. The exchange with Hussein looks familiar, but not all encounters follow this pattern. What if Hussein walked away as though you weren't there? How do you feel when your warm and friendly greeting is ignored? You may attribute a motive: have I said something wrong, is it me?

We know, from personal experience, how important it is to be acknowledged and appreciated. I think this is the essence of inclusion. Our well-being and sense of belonging can be compromised when our hunger for recognition goes unmet. The psychiatrist Sir Michael Rutter showed how vital recognition and attachment are to our development and flourishing.[7] So, a stroke is like offering and receiving a slice of recognition cake. Like a cake, sometimes it's too sickly and unpleasant; sometimes it's delicious and fulfilling. How strokes are exchanged affects our relationships, and stroking patterns can express aspects of workplace culture. While strokes are verbal and non-verbal, in this chapter I am focusing on verbal strokes.

How you offer and receive strokes will be part of the tone you set as a leader coach. When you are predictable, clear and inclusive with your strokes, colleagues feel safer. Your strokes can be positive or negative, conditional or unconditional. Here are some examples:

- **Positive Conditional:** 'Your arrangements for the away day were detailed and complete, thanks.'
- **Positive Unconditional:** 'Maria, you're such fun to work with.'
- **Negative Conditional:** 'I didn't like the lunch choices for the away day.'
- **Negative Unconditional:** 'You're rubbish.'

Start to notice the stroke patterns in your workplace. It can be revealing. I worked in a team with a leader whose strokes felt plastic and synthetic. Her intention was generous and kind. She affirmed everyone continually to build a positive working environment, ignoring some of the problems and tensions. We began to reject or ignore the strokes and distrust her motives. Our recognition and appreciation were overfed with too much sickly cake. Her praise and affirmations started to sound disingenuous. The ratio of positive to negative was unbalanced.

There is evidence from the positive psychology field that explains some of this.[8] In tests, when positive and negative comments were offered in ratio of around 3:1, team members responded effectively to criticism with more resilience. With too much positivity, ratios above 12:1, performance levels fell. The research suggests this applies to groups and individuals.

What does this mean for you as a leader coach? Careful attention to the stroking language you use has a significant impact. Find the appropriate balance and avoid negative, unconditional strokes, which belittle and discount the person or group. Reflect on what message is expressed in your strokes and be transparent and intentional. Here are some tips with regard to strokes to help you do this:

- Pay close attention to the nature of the strokes you give, receive and notice.

- Notice patterns with individuals and across groups.

- What culture is created where positive strokes are under-nourished and negative ones overfed?

- Who, in your team, refuses to give themselves positive strokes, or accept them from others?

- Who comes to you searching for strokes, seeking your approval for their work?

- Conditional strokes invite learning. Nourish conditional strokes to change the experience of 'feedback'. For example:
  o 'Your calculation in the summary is wrong', versus 'You can't add up'.
  o 'I feel uncomfortable when you shout', versus 'You make me feel uncomfortable when you shout'.

- Express specifically what you value about work and people with the same intensity and information you give to criticism. Then negative conditional strokes are equally valuable learning and part of the whole stroke economy.

- Be aware of culture. It may be impolite to offer even negative conditional strokes, certainly in public. Elsewhere, over-adapted politeness is equally unwelcome.

The language of discounting

My colleague, Leila, won an industry award for an outstanding piece of work. Many hands contributed, but it was her leadership that shaped it, marshalled the resources, and created the team. She was the creative force, and her influence was significant. She earned the recognition. I asked what the award meant to her. She replied with her characteristic pattern, one you may recognize in yourself and others. Her words revealed her habit of mind and behaviour. 'Well, you know I didn't do much really,' she said, 'it was the team that did the work. They're the important ones. I just...' shrugging her shoulders, as if she were shrugging off the positive stroke.

One way to describe this language is discounting and when you are familiar with it you will notice how common it is. I referred to it earlier as the preliminary invitation into games.

The behaviour is often out of awareness. It's a process in which people diminish or exaggerate aspects of themselves, others or reality. The theory was developed through observation and research in several psychology fields. For example, transactional analyst Jacqui Schiff, called it discounting.[9] A similar perspective is described in cognitive behavioural coaching practice as distorted thinking.[10] The origins of the behaviour are in our upbringing and ongoing development, like those aspects explored in Chapters 1 and 3 in this book. The behaviours are reinforced by repeating the pattern. It's like a script template of a play we never stop performing and it has the same ending each time. Discounting is a mosaic of recurring thinking, feeling and behaviour, with more dimensions than can be addressed here. So, my aim to is to offer some broad themes and examples for you to observe in yourself and others.

Example 1: How your team works together

As a leader coach, observe how your team works together on a task. Are they working effectively, or are they exhausted yet not achieving very much? Are they avoiding tasks? These can all be signs of discounting. The person denies or ignores relevant information and approaches relationships and issues from an internal frame of reference. For example, I may diminish my own culpability or contribution to an event and exaggerate the role of others, or vice versa, as illustrated in Leila's story above. Discounting may concern solving problems, or perceived problems. For example, you notice a colleague fails to address an important issue and discounts the significance, 'Well, it's no big deal really, everything will turn out fine.'

Example 2: When people discount their own behaviour

It's useful to develop the ability to name when people discount their own or others' behaviour. For example, I knew a leader who discounted his bullying behaviour by justifying it to himself and others, 'Well, people know what I'm like. They know I don't mean it. It isn't personal.' He'd admit, 'I know I can be difficult. I'm blunt, but that's just how I am and I'm not going to change now.' He wore what he called 'bluntness' as a badge of honour. I often hear leaders discount their impact on others, describing their behaviour as 'direct' or 'blunt', when in fact they are discounting, belittling and threatening. As a leader coach you call out that behaviour because you understand the difference between inclusive, assertive language and discounting.

Example 3: Avoidance of responsibility

You'll also notice those colleagues who avoid taking responsibility for their own thoughts, feelings and behaviour. For example, they say, 'I feel angry, and I can't help it.' The implication being, 'if you don't like my behaviour, don't blame me', followed by another common discounting expression, 'just get over it'. Listen out for people who discount their ability to think and change, for example, the person who over-invests in guilt and passively denies their ability to act, 'I wish I hadn't got so angry with him, but he just drives me mad. The worst thing is there's nothing I can do about it.'

Table 5.2 highlights some of the more common discounting words you're likely to hear, along with the underlying, implicit message that's given and what's being discounted.

Table 5.2   Spotting and interpreting discounting language

Discounting words	Example	Implicit message(s)	What's being discounted
Just	'I'm so sorry to bother you. I know you're really, really, busy, but I just wanted to ask if you could possibly...' or 'I'm just contacting you about...'	'I'm not important...' 'My needs aren't important' 'I hope to manipulate you to do what I want'	Discounting my importance, needs, existence
But	'Yes, you have a point, but you haven't...' or 'I really respect what you're saying but...'	'I don't respect your point really; my point is more important'	Discounting others (whatever comes before 'but')
Never	'You never listen...' 'I never get the breaks...'	'You're not listening now' 'You're not agreeing with me' 'Poor me'	Exaggerating reality ('never')
Can't	'I really can't stand it any longer...' 'There's no point, I just can't do it...'	'I'm stuck' 'I won't do it' 'I don't want to'	Discounting capacity to choose and act
Always	'You're always interrupting me...' 'Why does this always happen to me?'	'I'm a victim'	Exaggerating reality Discounting self Discounting others
Everyone	'Everyone thinks they're rubbish...' 'Everyone knows...' 'Everyone likes football...'	'I feel OK when I think people agree' 'I don't belong'	Exaggerating reality Discounting others
No one	'No one in our department thinks they're any good...' 'No one likes to do that...'	'Please, collude with me' 'I don't like it/them/us, etc' 'I don't belong'	Exaggerating reality Discounting others

(continued)

Table 5.2 (Continued)

Discounting words	Example	Implicit message(s)	What's being discounted
Should	'People should know how to behave…'	'My parents always told me…'	Discounting myself Discounting others You don't belong
Must	'I must stop procrastinating…'	'I don't want to…'	Discounting options and choice
Ought	'Well, she really ought to know better…' 'I ought to deal with his poor performance…'	'Things aren't how I want them to be'	Discounting others Discounting self
Could	'Yes, I suppose I could…'	'…but I probably won't'	Discounting agency and options

Table 5.3 Ways to respond to distorted thinking

Distorted thinking	Language example	Possible responses
All or nothing statements	'Tony *always* arrives late.' 'He just doesn't get it.' 'She's utterly *useless*/completely *brilliant*.' 'They *never* listen.'	'What doesn't he get?' 'Do you really mean always?' 'So, there's absolutely no hope for her?' 'Do you mean listen or agree?' 'Would you like to talk about this?'
Catastrophizing	'It's going to be a *disaster/brilliant*.' 'This is the *worst* thing ever.'	'Is it really the worst?' 'How might we be disappointed?' 'What might go well?' 'Would you like to talk about this?'
Should(n't)/must(n't)/ ought(n't)/can't	'He/I *should* deal with the problem.' 'They *ought* to know better.' 'I *must* speak to my colleague.' 'I simply *can't* work with him any longer.'	'When you say you can't, what's stopping you?' 'Who says you must?' 'When you say can't, do you mean won't?' 'Would you like to talk about this?'

Table 5.3   (Continued)

Distorted thinking	Language example	Possible responses
Blame	'You *know* what they're like.' 'Well, we all *know* whose *fault* it is.' 'If it weren't for him, this team would be great.'	'I don't know…' 'Who do you mean by *all*?' 'What is he representing on behalf of the whole group?' 'Would you like to talk about this?'
Predictions and attributions	'Well, I just *know* that's what they were thinking.' 'It's clear they are planning to close our department.' 'He really cares for *only* himself.' 'I *know/knew* I wouldn't get that job.'	'How do you know…?' 'What is the evidence for that?' 'What makes you say that?' 'Would you like to talk about this?'

Once you've strengthened your awareness and ability to spot discounting, you can respond in a way that addresses what has been discounted. Table 5.3 shows some useful responses to address distorted thinking. This is not an exhaustive list; it highlights the responses that I've found most useful and productive.

I also suggest a more effective way to respond, which doesn't require questions – to reflect back to the person what you hear and notice, and what is evoked in you. You may find this feels more benign yet is as effective. In response to 'I know/knew I wouldn't get that job', you might reflect, 'So, when you applied for the job, it was already in your mind that you weren't going to get it?' Often as they hear themselves, through you, awareness is raised.

There are some other common discounts I want to share:

- Discounting the significance of behaviour: 'I don't know what you're so bothered about, I'm not late very often'.

- Discounting the need to rest and recuperate, after sickness or working long hours: 'No, I'm OK thanks, I'm very resilient and not very tired really, not in the scheme of things', said with a sigh.

- Replacing the word 'I' with the word 'you', discounting their thoughts and feelings: 'Well, you've just got to get on with it haven't you? That's what you do when you're a leader, you're paid to deal with these problems and the stress'.

- The 'gallows laugh': 'Well, I really messed up there, ha ha ha', 'I had a bit of an accident, ha ha ha'. Essentially, a dissonant relationship between behaviour, laughing and what is said.

Discounting is pervasive. We all do it, so you won't have to look hard to find it. Once you begin to spot these patterns in the words people speak, use the questions and responses outlined here to encourage colleagues to take ownership for thoughts, feelings and actions, and to strengthen effective and productive work relationships.

Let's look at one more language pattern that you may be familiar with, and what you can do about it: redefining.

Redefining

I felt exasperated with a colleague. Our conversations lasted an age. We got nowhere. I felt uncertain, annoyed and misunderstood. We were stuck and I didn't know how to respond effectively. Only later, did I notice his habit of avoiding questions or answering from an unrelated perspective. You can identify the behaviour easily enough. Listen to politicians, they do this with journalists so often! You have a sense that you're being blocked or taken on a tangent. For example:

You: Are you going to talk to Brad about his behaviour as we've discussed before?

Colleague: Yes, I am certainly thinking about it.

You: As you think about it, how can you find a way to have the conversation that you are comfortable with?

Colleague: Well, it's not what I am comfortable with, but when I can find time.

You: Will you do it by the end of the week please?

Colleague: Well, you know how hard it is here to follow HR procedure.

You: So, what do you need to know about procedure to do what we've agreed before?

Colleague: Well, what I've tried to do up to now is…

If these shifts in conversations sound familiar, you've experienced redefining. You think your enquiry is clear and reasonable, your colleague finds it stressful in some way and discounts their capacity to respond appropriately. Your question may touch a psychological boundary, and they feel threatened. They may discount their ability to answer or ask for help. They may experience fear and feel vulnerable, they may have an over-adapted desire to please you. So, out of awareness, they divert you from the issue and defend themselves against a perceived threat. The threat may not be real, but it feels real for them! You'll know when it happens because you find you're going round in circles without getting anywhere.

To spot redefining, look out for when the purpose of your question is avoided by disagreeing about that purpose, definitions or the issue itself. You're diverted into a detailed discussion about the issue without finding an answer. You may become so confused that you doubt yourself and decide to meet again to discuss it further! You experience shifting sands as though you're going round in circles. This doesn't just happen at work; it can easily occur with friends and family as well. Table 5.4 gives some more examples you might be familiar with from your personal life.

Table 5.4 Redefining examples

You	Friend	Outcome
'What shall we do this weekend?'	'I'm so exhausted.'	You don't find a shared, satisfactory answer
'Do you like him?'	'Well, it depends on what you mean by "like".'	You still don't know if they like him
'What's your decision on the venue for the party?'	'It depends on who we're inviting.'	The party doesn't happen

Table 5.5   Questions to help step out of unproductive patterns

You	Colleague	Questions to step out of the pattern
'Are you going to talk to Brad about his behaviour as we've discussed before?'	'Yes, I am certainly thinking about it.'	'What's getting in the way of doing it?' 'I notice you are still thinking about it.' 'You sound hesitant/ concerned to me.' 'What do you need from me right now?'
'As you think about it, how can you find an effective way to resolve it that feels comfortable for you to do it?'	'Well, it's not what I am comfortable with, but when I can find time.'	'We seem to be stuck on this. What needs to happen for us to unstick this?' 'I notice you shifted from feeling comfortable with doing it, to time pressures. What's really going on for you?'

So, as a leader coach, how can you step out of these unproductive, cyclical conversations, with due care and kindness? In Table 5.5 are some alternative questions to ask to break the unproductive pattern.

It's important to check out your own thoughts and feelings in the moment so you are aware of what you bring to the conversation. How are you contributing to the stuck conversation? Perhaps you're feeling angry and that's evoking fear in your colleague. As a leader coach, here are some examples of questions to step out of the cycle of redefining:

- I notice we're angry with each other and I want to have a conversation which is mutually productive, so would you be willing to start again?
- I think we are stuck and going round in circles. How can we make progress?

- What do you need from me to make progress with this? What are you willing to do to help the process?
- We seem to be stuck. What's really concerning you about my request?

For you as a leader coach, understanding redefining dialogue gives you indispensable insights. When you notice the behaviour, you can change how you word your responses and step out of the cycle. Be kind to yourself and others; this behaviour is common to all of us some of the time.

Final thoughts

As you read in Chapter 3, as a leader coach you're always developing and learning. When you aim to be present and attend mindfully to the language used at work, you enter a world of endless opportunities for experiment and learning. I believe that when you care about how words make worlds, you become a stronger leader coach, more trusted, more respected, more effective. When you're straightforward in your language, enquire into the meaning-making of others, and when your language is clear about what you stand for, others know where they stand with you. When you're curious to learn what others stand for, you're open to find meaningful and mutually productive ways to work together. Your use of language is central to this process. As a refined leader coach friend of mine says: take Frank and Grace with you into every conversation – be frank, with grace.

Now that we've explored the power of language, the next chapter explores how to notice and shift unhelpful patterns of thinking and behaviour.

References

1 Berne, E (1964) *Games People Play*, Penguin, London
2 James, J (1973) The game plan, *Transactional Analysis Journal*, 3 (4), 14–17

3 Perls, F, Hefferline, R and Goodman, P (1951) *Gestalt Therapy: Excitement and growth in the human personality*, Delta, New York

4 Senge, P (2006) *The Fifth Discipline: The art and practice of the learning organisation*, Random House, London

5 Karpman, S (2012) Listening, learning, and accountability: Three rules of openness, three rules of accountability, and the adult scales, listening scales, and listener's loops, *Transactional Analysis Journal*, 42 (1), 71–86

6 Berne, E (1964) *Games People Play*, Penguin, London

7 Moursund, J (1985) Contact, intimacy, and need, *Transactional Analysis Journal*, 15 (2), 116–19

8 Losada, M and Heaphy, E (2004) The role of positivity and connectivity in the performance of business teams: A nonlinear dynamics model, *American Behavioral Scientist*, 47 (6), 740–65

9 Schiff, J L (1975) *Cathexis Reader: Transactional analysis treatment of psychosis*, Harper and Row, New York

10 Neenan, M and Dryden, W (2006) *Cognitive Behavioural Therapy: An A-Z of persuasive arguments*, John Wiley & Sons, London

Further reading

Fredrickson, B L and Losada, M F (2005) Positive affect and the complex dynamics of human flourishing, *American Psychologist*, 60 (7), 678–86

James, M (1975) *The OK Boss*, Addison-Wesley Publishing Company, Reading, MA

Napper, R (2009) Positive psychology and transactional analysis, *Transactional Analysis Journal*, 39 (1), 61–74

Schein, E (2013) *Humble Inquiry: The gentle art of asking instead of telling*, Berret-Koehler, San Francisco, CA

Sills, C (Ed) (2006) *Contracts in Counselling and Psychotherapy*, Sage Publications, London

Stewart, I and Joines, V (1987) *TA Today: A new introduction to transactional analysis*, LifeSpace Publishing, Nottingham

Shifting stuck thinking and behaviour

6

DENA PARIS

As a leader coach, how often have you felt that one of your team members or teams is stuck in their thinking or unhelpful behaviours? They seem to be spinning in place and not able to move forward. Regardless of the coaching or guidance you give, the same issues arise week after week, and they seem unable to get unstuck.

Unproductive patterns and habits can stall or even stop individuals and teams from reaching their full potential and achieving their goals and those of the organization. As a leader coach, being able to identify and then help shift these behaviours and ways of thinking can have a significant impact on the overall success of the individual, team and organization.

When these situations arise, you may wonder:

- How do I know when someone is stuck?
- How do I help shift unproductive behaviours and thinking?
- How am I contributing to stuck patterns?

Chapter 5 explored awareness of language as a leader coach; how the words people use can be clues to what's going on at a deeper level. This chapter looks at stuck patterns of behaviour, exploring the questions above and providing insights for how you can use your leader coach skills to get things moving again. To bring this to life we'll look at the fictionalized story of Neha and Michael, and how Neha helped Michael to get unstuck and make progress with an important strategic initiative.

How do you know when someone is stuck?

Neha, a successful senior leader in a global organization, was getting frustrated with Michael, a senior leader on her team. Michael had been on her team for several years, and he was always someone she could rely upon. Because of this, she had put him as the lead on a new, highly visible and important initiative. However, she felt Michael wasn't making much progress on the work and after each weekly check-in she was becoming more and more concerned they weren't going to meet the deadline. It seemed that each discussion was the same, Neha asking how the initiative was progressing and Michael responding it was 'fine' and then giving a quick update on the seemingly trivial actions he and the team had taken.

For about four weeks, Neha and Michael replayed this same discussion in their weekly check-ins. Neha wasn't sure what was happening other than the project was falling further and further behind, and her frustrations and concerns were increasing. What she didn't realize was that Michael was stuck.

When an individual is stuck, there is typically one or more contributing internal factors leading to them being in this position. These might include such things as core values being challenged, aspirations or motivations not being met, fear of failure, rejection or embarrassment. It can be difficult to understand or identify these areas given they are not usually voiced or visible. However, they typically manifest themselves into behaviour.

Luckily, as a leader coach, you are in a unique position to observe these behaviours given your front row seat to many of the actions of your team and team members. Even with this prime seat, you can miss the signs and clues that an individual or team is stuck if you aren't clear on what to look for. Learning to spot these behaviours allows you to help colleagues recognize, understand and make choices about how to shift the actions and habits that are contributing to them being stuck.

In Table 6.1 you will find a set of typical behaviours that might be exhibited by someone who is stuck. For each behaviour you will also find a set of questions to help you reflect on the situation.

Table 6.1 Behavioural signs of being stuck

Behaviour	Questions to reflect upon
Procrastination	Do they seem to put other activities first? Do they point to external reasons for the inaction? Are they focused on more trivial activities ('busy work')?
Overthinking	Is there constant need for more data or analysis? Do you get the sense of 'analysis paralysis'? Are they regularly weighing pros and cons?
Indecisiveness	Are decisions hard for them to make? Do they look to you or others to make the decisions? Are deadlines missed?
Lack of focus	Is prioritization difficult for them? Are they spending time and energy on work that is trivial or could be done by someone with less experience? Do they seem to be bouncing from idea to idea, finding it hard to land?
Lack of knowledge	Do they seem confused? Do you frequently hear them say 'I don't know', 'I'm not sure' or something similar? Is their work product below expectations?
Discussion avoidance	Are difficult or uncomfortable conversations being avoided? Are there meetings after meetings? (Pay particular attention to this in team dynamics.)
Repeated patterns	Are the same solutions and approaches being used repeatedly regardless of previous outcomes or current situations? Do they use the same reasoning and rationale repeatedly?
Disengagement	Are they less interested or enthusiastic? Do they seem aloof or 'somewhere else' during discussions?
Emotional reactiveness	Is feedback met with resistance or dismissiveness? Do they blame others?

Pay particular attention to any shifts in behaviours. Are these new? Different? If yes, then you will want to jump in quickly and learn what is leading to these new behaviours. Acting quickly prevents the situation from festering and becoming a significant issue. Even when these behaviours have been present for a longer period, you still have an opportunity to shift the pattern to one which is healthier and more productive, so don't delay.

How to help shift unproductive behaviours and thinking

Neha and Michael's story continues.

Michael was exhibiting a few of these external signs… procrastination, work not getting done, lack of focus and lack of knowledge. These were new and Neha had not seen them from Michael in the past, so she was confused. What was happening? Why was he failing? What did she need to do? Neha had a choice and decision to make about how to progress the work, and how best to address Michael's performance and help get him unstuck. There were several potential options she felt she could take to manage the situation, all of which she had deployed in similar situations in the past with other employees. While all of these were viable options, she knew there were both positive and negative outcomes that came with each approach:

- **Take over:** She could step in and take over the work she had asked Michael to do. This would ensure the work was progressing and done to her liking; however, it could very easily lead to her becoming overburdened with the additional work. This approach could also create new problems given she would need to deprioritize other work that was just as impactful on the organization.

- **Reassign the work:** She could give the initiative to someone else on her team and remove Michael from the work completely. This would be quick and easy but, while tempting, she could unintentionally send a message not only to Michael, but to others on her team that failure is not an option, you must be perfect and growth is unimportant.

- **Demote:** She could bring in someone more senior than Michael who she knew could get the work done and hope that Michael would learn from that person. While this would most likely lead to the work being done it could lead to Michael feeling inadequate, not trusted, embarrassed or myriad other emotions. This could also miss an opportunity for the more senior individual to learn new skills and stretch their capabilities, as well as stunting Michael's growth and limiting the capabilities of the team overall.

- **Be directive:** She could tell Michael what to do, how to do it and when to do it. Again, this could ensure the work was done her way, but it could create a pattern in which Michael and other members of her team could become reliant upon her to 'rescue' them when there is discomfort, or things become difficult. Again, this would overburden Neha and deny Michael an opportunity for growth.

In addition to the drawbacks above, each of these options create an environment lacking in psychological safety. Thought leader in the field of psychological safety, Amy Edmondson, writes that 'Psychological safety exists when people feel their workplace is an environment where they can speak up, offer ideas, and ask questions without fear of being punished or embarrassed.' 'It is not about being nice,' but rather 'about candor and making it possible for productive disagreement and free exchange of ideas… It is not about lowering performance standards.'[1]

As someone who understood and believed in the importance of creating a psychologically safe environment for her team, Neha knew clearly that these options would not benefit her, Michael or the organization. These actions would jeopardize the environment she had been creating since taking on the role. If she took over the work, removed Michael or put someone over him it would demonstrate to him that he could not speak up or make a mistake without being punished or embarrassed. However, she didn't know what to do instead or what was really happening. Was it Michael? Was it the work? Was it how she was giving direction? Was there something else she wasn't seeing?

Neha started to become curious.

Shifting to curiosity

Curiosity is about enquiring, learning and understanding. Fully embracing a curious mindset can provide the entry point into understanding and then shifting unproductive behaviours and ways of thinking. Curiosity is at the heart of coaching. When you are curious, it is nearly impossible to be judgemental or directive. It opens the space for the other person to learn and create new ways of approaching situations. It also helps you to shine some light on the internal factors contributing to current behaviours and ways of thinking. Curiosity can lead to greater clarity on the 'why' behind behaviour. Here are some questions you can ask yourself to move into a more curious frame of mind:

- How can I best understand what's going on here?
- What am I not seeing?
- What might I be missing?
- What might this person be experiencing?
- Is 'that' true? How do I know it's true? ('That' can be any assumption or belief.)
- What assumptions am I making?

Perspective shifting – the balcony and the dance floor

> Embracing her curiosity and resisting her urge to solve, resolve and fix, Neha shifted her focus onto Michael. She wanted to understand more about him and the current situation but was finding it difficult to see something new. She knew she needed a different perspective.

Stepping back and seeing the whole picture can be both powerful and challenging. As a leader, you tend to be in the action. To get that perspective, Ronald Heifetz and Marty Linsky suggest the metaphor of getting off the dance floor and going to the balcony to allow you step back during the action and see the whole picture.[2,3]

The image of a dance floor and balcony offers a useful way to visualize the fluidity with which, as a leader coach, you can shift between different perspectives – moving seamlessly between the big picture and the individual parts.

Continuing with this metaphor, being on the balcony, even if for only a short period of time, affords you the opportunity to see all of what is happening on the dance floor. You can see more clearly the movements and patterns that are difficult, if not impossible, to recognize when you are in the dance, seeing only that which is nearest you. When on the dance floor you can experience the activities and music. When on the balcony you are better able to see not only the individual pieces, but the sum of the parts.

Moving between the dance floor and the balcony at the right time and with the right balance between the two is a skill. Too much time above can lead to being too removed to affect change. Too much time below can lead to missing important insights and getting swept up in the action, especially during intense or stressful times. Finding a useful balance will allow you to observe where there might be issues and then exploring, in detail, with others what you saw and what they are experiencing.

When on the dance floor it can be difficult to identify the coachable moments with your team members and what is influencing certain behaviours. When you get swept up in the moment of solving, resolving and fixing the problems around you and the team, it is hard to step out of the action. This is when it is important to take a moment, walk up the stairs to the balcony and observe with curiosity what is occurring.

To move from the dance floor to the balcony and back again, you must first start with the recognition that a change in perspective would be helpful. Once this has happened, visualize walking off the dance floor and over to a staircase leading up to the balcony. Walk up the stairs and when you get to the top turn and look down on the dance floor. Imagine seeing the individual(s) who is (are) at the centre of the situation. Widen the aperture. What else do you see or notice? Try looking at it all through the eyes of someone seeing this dance floor and the people dancing for the first time ever. What do you see? Use the curiosity questions given earlier. You may notice something right away or it may take some time. Be patient and allow your curiosity to guide your attention.

Neha did this visualization. She went to the balcony. She embraced a curious mindset. She observed what was happening through a fresh set of eyes. The first thing she noticed was Michael's procrastination, which was not typical for him. He was usually on top of all his work and meeting deadlines without issue. It also became clearer that he was spinning his wheels when it came to the first phase of the work, which was research and analysis. The more she observed, the more curious she became about what was behind these new behaviours for Michael. Her initial reaction was to write the story herself, to explain why these behaviours were showing up. The story would have included such things as 'He's so busy', 'His team isn't pulling their weight', 'He doesn't love this type of work', etc. But instead of expending energy on assumptions, she decided to go to the source and find what was at the root of the behaviours. This meant speaking with Michael.

She moved back down to the dance floor and began to explore with Michael. Neha started the discussion by sharing her concerns about the lack of progress of the work, that she was curious about what was happening and her hopes of exploring the situation with him. Some of the questions she asked Michael during the discussion included:

- What are your thoughts?
- What is currently getting in the way of the work progressing?
- If you could change one thing about the situation, what would it be?
- How are you feeling about the work?

She then allowed Michael's responses and reactions to steer where they then went next in the discussion. Not moving into the discussion with a set agenda, but rather with a genuine desire to learn more, she opened the space for true exploration. She avoided asking directive questions so the discussion could remain open and really get to the truth of what was happening. She asked him open-ended questions, which lead to open thinking. She focused on him and the experience he was having with this work and not the work itself. She recalled something she read that stated 'coach the person, not the problem'. She also tried to suspend her assumptions and opinions to truly listen to him and his experience with this initiative. She told herself to act similarly to a scientist, embodying curiosity, observation and neutrality.

Asking questions about someone's experience rather than the work itself is an important distinction. It is very easy to get curious about the topic or issue. Collecting facts and data typically indicate you are arming yourself with the information needed to solve the problem, or at least the perceived problem, for the other person. As was discussed in Chapter 2, this is normal for many leaders, and you might recognize this habit in yourself. You have been rewarded again and again for solving problems. As such, your first instinct might be to figure out the problem and find the solution. What you may want to consider is how you might use this problem-solving strength differently. Imagine using it to focus on the person and how to help them unlock their thinking and strengths to find the solution to the problem. This means shifting from focusing on the problem to focusing on the person. You are still using your skills and experience, but they are being used in a different way.

Neha could have easily shared with Michael all the issues she thought were getting in the way. She could have then shared the solutions to those issues. Instead, she focused on him and through curious enquiry and deep listening, uncovered for them both what was at the root of the issue. She contributed a few ideas to the discussion but always shifted back to Michael and his reactions to the ideas. This back and forth between coaching and contributing allowed Neha to be a part of finding a solution by tapping into her experience and expertise but at the same time allowing Michael to own the process and solution. Neha was able to share what she had observed and then moved into questions about Michael's experience with this initiative. She would learn later that the issues leading him to be stuck had never even crossed her radar. If she had tried to fix this for him, she would have been wasting time solving an issue that wasn't causing the problem!

Neha drew on her skills and experience as a leader coach to help Michael get unstuck and make progress. Table 6.2 highlights some coaching techniques and reminders that can support you in your conversations with colleagues and team members.

Table 6.2 Leader coach skills to help someone get unstuck

Questioning		
	Use open-ended questions	What is happening?
		What impact is this having on you?
		What concerns/fears do you have?
		What might be in your way of moving forward?
		What is within your control? What isn't?
		What constraints are there? How might you overcome these?
		How would you like to move forward?
		What support do you need? How will you get that support?
	Only ask genuine questions	Don't ask if you don't care
		Don't ask if you know the answer
		Don't ask if you are going to tell them what to do anyway
	Don't disguise advice as a question	Have you thought about doing...?
		Have you tried...?
	Don't ask leading questions	How long have you been unhappy?
		Are you falling behind because of... (insert options)?
	Avoid 'why'	Why did you do it that way?
		Why didn't you do this earlier?
		Note: In many cultures 'why' can feel judgemental
	Ask one more question than you think you need... you'll be amazed what will emerge	

Listening	Listen deeply and with curiosity
	Listen for what is not being said
	Listen beyond facts
	Listen empathetically
Name it	Share what you are noticing – from the balcony, the dance floor and in the moment
Impact/importance	Explore the impact of the current behaviour or way of thinking on them, others and the work
	Ask what would happen if nothing changed
Focus	Focus on the person, not on the topic or issue

Neha asked questions, focusing not on solving the problem for Michael, but instead on what the problem was for him. She fought the urge to fix the situation, by staying curious and keeping in mind that he was resourceful, creative, capable and in the best position to find a solution. She learnt that he wanted to do the work but was unclear how to move forward given this work had more 'white space' than he had anticipated. The scope of work was not as narrowly defined as previous initiatives, and it could have taken many different paths, which was leading to him feeling overwhelmed and lost. In turn, he was struggling to give direction to his team since he wasn't clear on where the work should go.

Through his discussion with Neha, and the reflections that arose from her questions, he gained clarity on what the blockers were for him. These included a fear of failure, and applying the same approach to this work as he had to almost all other past projects, even though this initiative required more innovation and planning. Once he recognized this, he was able to create a new plan to tackle the work. He decided to bring the key members together and co-create the path forward rather than doing it autonomously.

Before this conversation, Michael knew he was struggling with the initiative but wasn't sure why, or how to 'fix' the situation. He felt he was letting Neha down as well as his team. He was also not used to feeling this way given his historically strong performance and successes. He was not used to 'failing' and he wasn't able to move into action. He was essentially paralysed due to fear. He left the discussion with Neha feeling relieved, empowered and re-energized, as well as with a plan he was able to create. After the discussion, both Neha and Michael felt better, and the project started to move ahead.

Neha took time afterwards to reflect upon what had occurred. She noted that if she had chosen one of her other options (for example taking over, reassigning the work, demoting, being directive) it wouldn't have got to the root of the problem. The delays would have most likely continued, and Michael would have felt less psychologically safe and missed an opportunity to learn. Neha would have been overwhelmed with the additional work (short and long term), concerned about the deliverable, and frustrated with Michael, making her question his capabilities and what he could or couldn't take on in the future.

How are you contributing to stuck patterns?

It's essential to examine how your behaviour may be contributing to any stuck patterns for your team, and colleagues. You are part of a system. 'A system is a set of dynamically connected elements. If you do something to any one of those elements, the others are also affected.'[4] What any one person does in a system affects everyone else. You are a member of the system, and so your actions have an impact on it and the people in it, whether you are fully aware of it or not. It can be both interesting and productive to observe how you are contributing to situations when your team members are stuck. It is important not to underestimate your influence as the leader within the system. Given your power and position in the organization, within the team, and your one-to-one relationships, your impact in the system will most likely be amplified as compared to others.

Perceptual positions

Using the metaphor of the balcony and dance floor again, moving back up to the balcony is a great way to gain clarity on your role and impact. Perceptual positions is a methodology that can help you get there and to explore different perspectives once you've arrived.[5,6] You read an example of perceptual positions in Chapter 4, when a leader coach was struggling with one of their team who did not show up to work. Here, we explore this methodology in more detail to experience a situation from three different perspectives: self, other and observer.

- First position (self)
  - This is the position from which you see and hear the world through your own filters. It is where you stand in your own shoes and process situations through your own 'map of the world', values, emotions, beliefs and needs.
- Second position (other)
  - This position is where you see and hear the world through the eyes and ears of another. You stand in the other person's shoes and view the situation through their 'map of the world', values, emotions, beliefs and needs. This is the position from which you embrace empathy.

- Third position (observer)
  - This is the position of a neutral observer. It is taking on the role of the 'fly on the wall' to notice others and yourself through a more objective lens. In this position you can observe yourself, others and the relationship between all the people involved.

A fourth position, which is often useful, can be to take the perspective of the wider system. It explores how the dynamics between the self and observer are impacting others and the organizational context.

Moving between different positions can bring new insights, raise self-awareness and bring greater clarity. Practising this concept is simple and includes reflection, enquiry and curiosity. Figure 6.1 illustrates the flow of moving through the positions and reflective questions in each position. It is recommended that prior to moving to each position you clear your mind and take two or three deep, slow breaths. This will allow you to enter each position with fresh perspective. While in each position, it can be helpful to close your eyes as you consider each question.

Using the perceptual positions methodology

1 Begin with position 1, 'self'. Clear your mind and take two or three breaths. Imagine yourself in the situation as yourself. Ask yourself each of the questions for position 1. After considering each question reflect upon what emerged for you. What thoughts arose? What emotions arose? Where did you feel it in your body? Write down your reflections.

2 Now, repeat the same process for the next two positions, embodying the 'other' and impartial 'observer' roles as best you can.

3 After moving between these three positions, it can be very helpful to return to position 2 (other) and notice what might look different after having gone through all positions. Ask yourself the same questions and notice what arises.

4 Lastly, reflect upon what changes you might want to make in your behaviours and actions. What is there for you to learn? After doing this, move back to position 1 (self) and imagine you've applied these changes. Ask yourself the same questions and notice what is different.

Figure 6.1 Using perceptual positions

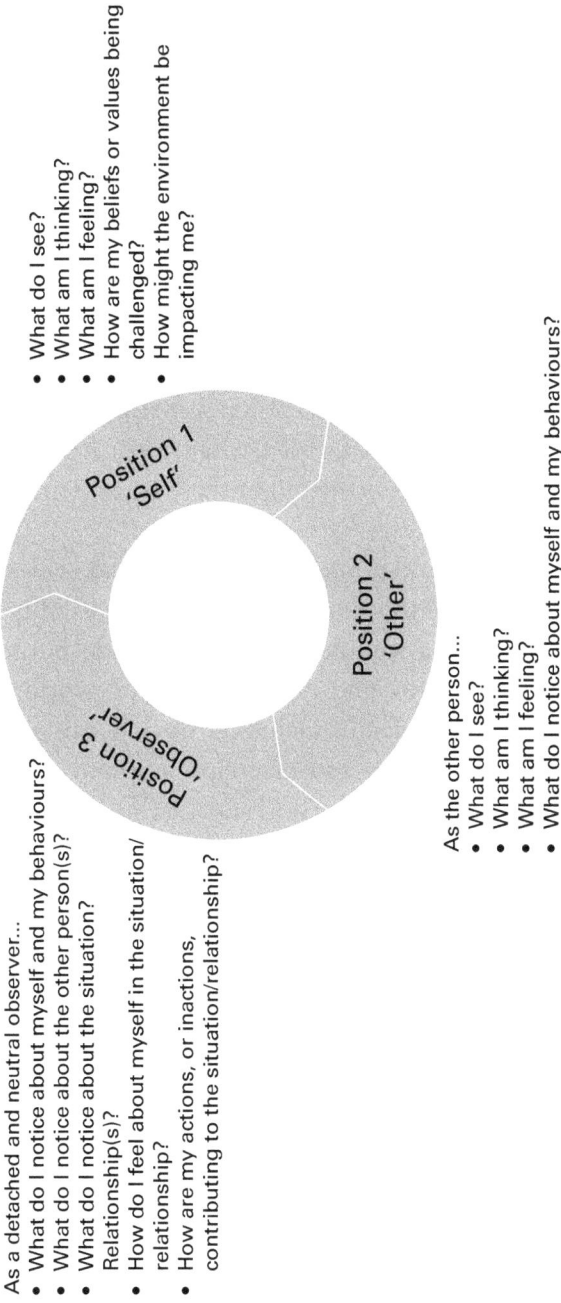

As a detached and neutral observer...
- What do I notice about myself and my behaviours?
- What do I notice about the other person(s)?
- What do I notice about the situation?
Relationship(s)?
- How do I feel about myself in the situation/relationship?
- How are my actions, or inactions, contributing to the situation/relationship?

Position 3
'Observer'

Position 1
'Self'

Position 2
'Other'

- What do I see?
- What am I thinking?
- What am I feeling?
- How are my beliefs or values being challenged?
- How might the environment be impacting me?

As the other person...
- What do I see?
- What am I thinking?
- What am I feeling?
- What do I notice about myself and my behaviours?

Once you've completed the full process, step back and review what you've written. Reflect on what you noticed in each position. You may want to observe yourself for a few days, with compassion and curiosity, and without judgement. What patterns do you see? What changes might you like to make in how you behave or interact with others?

You may have operated in a particular way for a long time and been quite successful because of it. Changing these behaviours, which have become ingrained habits, can be challenging and unnerving. It takes effort and awareness to recognize these habits and then even more effort to replace them with new behaviours. This type of change will take some courage. You have been rewarded for these behaviours over and over again and doing something different comes with a level of risk. Get curious about what might happen if you were to take that risk. What benefits might there be to you, others or the organization if you changed your behaviours?

You may also be the most experienced and senior person in the room. You may feel this comes with the responsibility to have all the answers, which is a significant and unrealistic burden to place on yourself in a complex and rapidly changing world. Chapter 2 explores this in more detail, including how it can significantly limit others' potential. If you embrace curiosity and assume every individual is resourceful, creative and capable, you can relieve yourself of the sense of responsibility to solve, resolve and fix everything. This creates a space for others to blossom, which can be liberating for you and empowering for others.

Neha experimented with perceptual positions. As she moved through each position, she jotted down what was coming up for her. From position 1 (self), she saw that Michael was flailing, the work wasn't getting done, and she was frustrated. What surprised her was that she was also feeling scared... scared that the work would fail, and her reputation would be on the line. She was also doubting her judgement. She was feeling that she might have assessed Michael and his capabilities incorrectly. She also realized that her core value of trust was being challenged. She had trusted him, and he was letting her down. In position 2, in Michael's shoes, she saw an overwhelming amount of work with little guidance. She saw that she (as the manager) wasn't providing much support, but instead was only asking about progress and reiterating the importance of the initiative. In Michael's shoes she felt frustrated, disappointed and fearful. When she moved to position 3 (observer), she saw two people not communicating very well. She saw herself as not being curious about what was happening for Michael and the team. She was just telling him to get the work done. She noticed Michael was struggling but not speaking up or sharing what was really happening. She saw that two people who typically worked well together were not connecting well on this work. Ultimately, she realized that she was allowing the situation to perpetuate by not really opening up the dialogue with Michael and exploring the situation with him. She saw the shift when she became curious, went up to the balcony, and started having real discussions with Michael. She saw him and the team becoming more engaged and empowered. She had been willing to consider how her behaviour was perpetuating the stuckness, and to take action to resolve this.

Final thoughts

People frequently get stuck in their organizational roles, which can limit their progress and their ongoing development. It can get in the way of individuals and teams reaching their potential and contributing positively to organizational performance. As a leader coach you are in a unique position to help them get unstuck if you are willing to be open and curious and put your coaching skills into practice. Trust that others are creative, resourceful and capable, and remove yourself from the action on the dance floor to go up to the balcony to gain new perspectives. This will help you to focus on the person, not just the topic or problem. Helping them explore what's in the way (acknowledging that sometimes it might be you) and finding different solutions can have a significant impact on the overall success of the individual, team and organization.

In the next chapter we shift our focus from one-to-one relationships and dynamics to how you can bring a coaching approach to leading teams.

References

1 Edmondson, A (2019) *The Fearless Organization: Creating psychological safety in the workplace for learning, innovation, and growth*, John Wiley and Sons, Hoboken, NJ

2 Heifetz, R (1998) *Leadership Without Easy Answers*, Harvard University Press, Cambridge, MA

3 Heifetz, R and Linsky, M (2017) *Leadership on the Line: Staying alive through the dangers of change*, Harvard Business School Press, Boston, MA

4 Ancona, D and Perkins, D N T (2022) Family ghosts in the executive suite, *Harvard Business Review*, January–February, https://hbr.org/2022/01/family-ghosts-in-the-executive-suite (archived at https://perma.cc/NQW2-S6C3)

5 Carroll, M (2008) Using perceptual positions, NLP Academy, 28 October, www.nlpacademy.co.uk/articles/view/using_perceptual_positions/ (archived at https://perma.cc/E9BT-P2PU)

6 Trainers Toolbox (nd) Perceptual positions: Powerful exercise to strengthen understanding and empathy, www.trainers-toolbox.com/perceptual-positions-powerful-exercise-to-strengthen-understanding-and-empathy/ (archived at https://perma.cc/URW7-PE4Z)

Leader coach as team leader 7

ANGELA RYAN

As a leader coach, you build your coaching skills and capabilities through developing the potential of your individual team members on a one-to-one basis. As this approach deepens and embeds, you will build greater confidence and capability with your coaching skills, and gain traction with your team members. At this juncture, many leader coaches then consider how to roll this coaching stuff out at scale, how to extend the scope of their coaching to impact every person that their role touches, and how to deploy coaching to further build individual, team and organizational potential.

This chapter will explore how you can do this – how to shift from coaching individuals to a team coaching approach. If this resonates with you, your objective now will be to expand your capabilities from impactfully coaching individuals to creating a coaching culture and outcomes across a team. In this chapter we'll investigate factors such as geography, culture and team dynamics, with some practical examples from the experiences of other global leader coaches. These factors should be considered in conjunction with the management and leadership development you have experienced to date in your career, as I seek to add to that knowledge, not replace it.

The pragmatic reality of operating as a leader within organizations often entails being faced with paradoxes inherent in the competing priorities of people and organizations. There are no easy solutions here, yet as a leader coach your ability to navigate this is crucially important. You will face moments when you need to give clear direction and manage underperformance rather than coach for potential. In Chapter 4, which focuses on your everyday role as a leader, we explored some frameworks that are useful in these often challenging situations. While you build potential within your team through coaching you still need to deliver performance and operational excellence. If you do not deliver on this, you will fail to achieve business outcomes. Being a leader coach means an evolution in the style with which you are now choosing to lead your team. Establishing your team coaching culture and systems must always be based on strong management foundations, otherwise you and they will sink.

> Chris was an enthusiastic internal coach; they had quickly accelerated through internal coaching programmes, and they prioritized this growth by adding external coaching accreditations and qualifications to their skill set. As they adapted to a coaching approach with their team, they sometimes did not fully manage them. This began to have underperformance implications for some members. Chris was able to reset this approach, to ensure that they started with management fundamentals and then overlaid this with targeted coaching opportunities with individuals who were ready for coaching.

You will need to create a bespoke approach, leveraging the skills and experience you have built during your management, leadership and coaching journeys, and integrate those into your current context. The starting point is one of self-reflection. Most likely, your own leadership development path will have involved thoughtful consideration. You will undoubtedly know your strengths and opportunities, so the next step is to map these to your team context and create your team leader coach strategy. If you have not yet completed this self-inventory, I would encourage you to return to Chapter 3 and explore your ongoing personal development. This chapter presumes that you have already developed core management skills such as goal setting and giving feedback to your direct reports. Here, we'll build on that foundation to help you accelerate your existing skills with a coaching approach for your team.

Geography and the leader coach

Where in the world were you born and raised? Do you now live and work in the same geography or have you moved? Do you travel frequently and are you responsible for team members in other locations?

As you calculate the readiness of your environment for your evolving team coaching approach, consider the geography in which you operate, organizational culture and your own sense of personal identity. These are the starting points to consider how to impact a team through your coaching skills and mindset. Every employee, including you, comes into the workplace as the outcome of their lived experience, the country culture they were raised in, their family upbringing, the educational and societal norms and expectations that shaped them during their formative times. Chapter 1 explored this with you and now we apply this to your team.

Looking more broadly at team leadership, the construct of a leader has very distinct stereotypes around the world. As you consider how to best lead your team/function or company with a coaching approach, you will need to anchor this around the geographical nuances for both you and your team members. If you operate in a multinational company then you may be leading across borders; perhaps you are living and working abroad, or you are a frequent traveller to other countries. Even if not cross-border it is highly likely that you will be leading across differing local cultures with the wonderful range and curiosities of social norms.

If you live and work where you grew up and your team is more homogenous, there will still be differences between the people in your team based on their upbringing, education and life stage. Diversity, equity, inclusion and belonging (DEI&B) are a leadership mandate, your role is to create the environment where everyone feels safe, that they belong and can reach their potential. Adopting a coaching approach can aid these endeavours. The diversity of your team, in whatever shape that takes, will require differing approaches from you and influence the underlying readiness of your team to engage with your approach as a leader coach.

National culture

The idea of a leader and the anticipated behaviours of someone holding a leadership role varies significantly around the world. National culture gives us a first clue: national culture refers to a system of deeply founded values, attitudes and behaviours of the members of a society, which we often define as being distinct to a country.[1] For example, if we take coaching in an organizational context, the practice predominately originated in the West and was based on western norms of management and leadership. However, even within those countries we define as western, there are significant differences in hierarchical norms and how decisions are made, which are the key markers of leadership. This is a significant consideration as you develop your coaching leadership profile and practice. Conflict can often arise from differences in communication styles, language barriers and unarticulated expectations.

There are some well-researched models you can refer to if you want to learn more about this. For example, Geert Hofstede's 1983 study remains the most notable model in the field of national culture, highlighting five dimensions of national culture found across 117,000 employees of IBM.[2,3,4] Project GLOBE (Global Leadership and Organizational Behaviour Effectiveness) further expanded Hofstede's five dimensions to nine dimensions.[5] The nine dimensions can be utilized by leader coaches to develop their teams best suited to the national culture. For example, an individualistic society such as the US or the UK may measure employee performance on individual achievement, whereas a communitarianism culture such as in Thai society may measure performance with a team goal-setting and coaching approach.

National cultures of different countries also give an insight into typical leadership behaviours. For example, a study on China and India reveals a higher power distance index, which means that people expect and respect hierarchical structure and authority.[6] The study further finds that national cultures result in different responses to differing management initiatives, for example, change projects are more successful when employees are involved in decision making in Estonia, but employee involvement has a negative effect in China and India.

So, what does this mean practically for you? Adopting a coaching style with a diverse team requires you to first understand the nuances and local expectations of a leader before you attempt to move everyone into a coaching-based relationship. You will need to recognize where your new approach may cause unintended consequences and confusion, as happened with the example of Beatrice.

Beatrice was a successful finance practitioner, and she was raised and predominately worked in the US. She was promoted to a global role based out of the US and was tasked with leading a virtual team across south-east Asia on a high-profile project. Coming from an environment that celebrated individual achievement and encouraged personal accountability, Beatrice had powered through her coaching training and was keen to use the approach with her team so that she could further develop their capabilities. Self-aware, she recognized south-east Asia was not her area of expertise and she was keen to learn from her team about the region.

She applied a coaching framework from day one, encouraging the team to find their own solutions to the deliverables and constantly asking for input and ideas. However, the team's nuance of leadership and office behaviour was different to what she was accustomed to, and she initially misinterpreted the reluctance to 'speak up' as meaning her team were lacking in ideas and even capabilities. Her team in turn described her in her 360-degree feedback as indecisive and some people complained that she would not give them clear direction. This muddle in expectations meant that deadlines started to be missed. Working with her own internal coach enabled Beatrice to approach the issue differently. She recognized the importance of meeting the needs her team required of her as a leader. She subsequently shifted her style of communication and set out a core management framework that clarified roles and responsibilities by each person in the team. She delegated problems for her team to solve and coached them collectively and individually. Agreeing these parameters with the team up front and acknowledging hierarchies meant she provided them with the requested certainty and clarity and was also able to progress her leader coach agenda.

How did Beatrice and her own coach practically determine how to move forward with the cultural variances? Erin Meyer conceptualized the Culture Map to assist organizations to build a greater understanding of how cultural patterns of belief and behaviour influence our perceptions, cognitions and actions.[7] The eight scales identified in his work were:

- communicating
- evaluating
- leading
- deciding
- trusting
- disagreeing
- scheduling
- persuading

These can enable the leader coach to examine how different cultures relate based on the relative position of two countries' culture to each other. Beatrice applied the model to her own context and that of her team.

I recommend this tool for the international leader coach, particularly to help you adapt to nuances of both leading and coaching your teams. Like Beatrice, this was a learning juncture in my own leader coach development. I realized that for some people, coaching (and therefore not providing all the answers) meant I was not fulfilling their basic requirements of leadership. From their perspective I was simply not being effective. My advice here is to not be disheartened if some of your team members don't initially share your enthusiasm for your coaching approach, particularly in parts of the world where coaching as a leadership style is still emerging. Be aware of cultural nuances and build sufficient flexibility into your range of leadership behaviours to ensure that you individualize your people's experience. Your role as a leader coach is to get the best from your people and build their potential; sometimes that means acknowledging that your evolving leader coach style may not (yet) be optimal for them. Indeed, you must always meet people where they are before you can accelerate.

Alignment with organizational culture

Once you have determined any implications of geographical culture you next need to take an internal view of your organizational culture. This broader concept will be further explored in Chapter 9 with specific focus on coaching culture. You need to identify the authentic values and behaviours that embody your organization's culture and explore the congruence, and indeed any dissonance, with your role as a leader coach. Your organizational cultural experience will depend upon location, industry and your seniority. At the level you operate at and the context you operate in, you will likely be juggling multiple perspectives, and your experience will differ from people at other levels. How would you describe the organizational culture that you operate in? I am sure that your organization website or office walls will have some cultural definitions and that there may be espoused values. But what does the organization *really* value?

Do you understand how your organization identifies and rewards both potential and performance? If the organization has a leadership model does this reflect and include coaching behaviours? For example, do management development programmes broadly build the skills and capabilities to both give and receive feedback? Does the organization actively create two-way discussions and provide employees with a voice? All these components are required for a coaching culture, and you need to understand whether shifting your leadership approach will feel misaligned with organizational culture.

If you are developing as a leader coach as part of a systemic organizational approach then you will likely have the benefit of skills, a shared mindset and internal resources to support you. If not, then you will need to identify systems, support and champions elsewhere in the organization or externally to support your ambitions. You may need a champion or sponsor if your role or seniority does not provide you with the agency to make the systemic changes. But even if your organization does not reflect a coaching culture, you can still create one with your team.

You and your team

As a leader coach and within the larger ecosystem of your organizational culture you will need to define and build a team culture that supports your coaching ambition. Trust, mindset and psychological safety will be foundations and are explored below. Once established you can then move to systemize your approach.

Trust comes first

If I were to ask your team members whether they trust you and feel trusted, how would they respond? Do they trust one another? Do you have any recent employee surveys or mechanisms that provide data about this? Trust is the principal cornerstone of all relationships and essential in creating a coaching culture with your team. Your team must feel trusting and trusted. If you currently have a low-trust environment, then you need to build this before you begin to introduce a coaching culture with your team.

Growth mindset

A mindset receptive to coaching is required by your team both individually and collectively. One example is the growth mindset. Carol Dweck, leading expert on mindset, motivation and achievement, developed this body of work around mindsets, applying how our ways of thinking define how we understand our own experiences.[8] In turn this determines our emotional, cognitive, behavioural and neural responses. Dweck further defined two mindset positions: fixed and growth, with research suggesting that those individuals exhibiting growth mindsets are the most likely to flourish by learning new skills and adapting, even during challenging times. She suggested that individuals hold different innate perceptions and reactions to learning and progress depending on their choice of mindset.

A growth mindset is a belief that one's basic intelligence and talent are flexible and changeable. Conversely, a fixed mindset is a belief that one's basic intelligence and talent are determined from birth and cannot be altered. Popular research advocates for the development of a growth mindset due to associated advantages that come with it, such as having a more open and positive perception of challenges as opportunities, and stronger resilience in the face of failure.[9] These are critical components for a team to embrace coaching, where ideas can be constructively explored, adopted or discounted.

What happens if members of your team do not currently have this mindset? Research suggests that individuals can be primed to believe and behave according to growth or fixed mindsets. Unfortunately, early life experiences can prime many individuals for a fixed mindset, which can limit their growth and learning in future life. The good news is that it is possible to reverse this phenomenon and as a leader coach you will are well placed to enable this shift.

Three pillars are required: self-efficacy (an individual's self-belief in their capability and chance of success), belief in free will and will-power. Organizations and leader coaches can implement structures to support a shift towards a growth mindset, and indeed coaching conversations are one brilliant tool that can be used to do so. Critically, however, the research shows that individual employees will need to learn any required mindset change directly from role models around them, and this includes you. So, the question becomes 'Which mindset do you operate from?'

Psychological safety

Psychological safety is the third essential component for the leader coach.

> The belief that one will not be punished or humiliated for speaking up with ideas, questions, concerns, or mistakes, and that the team is safe for interpersonal risk taking.[10]

Without a culture built on psychological safety your ambitions as a leader coach will not succeed. Psychological safety needs to exist in-dividually between all team members, as well as with you. You must nurture and protect the safety when individual team members' words or behaviour dent it. Once again, it starts with you. The way that you behave and speak to your team matters. Do you encourage dissenting views, listen to each one, respond without judgement, and encourage debate in your private and team meetings? Do you treat your people with respect both publicly and privately, even in the most challenging moments? Are you constructive and caring? Do your people feel that they matter, truly matter, as a human being rather than a 'human resource'? If you cannot answer these questions, then explore with your own coach or HR team how you can best diagnose your current team culture and understand how your people experience you as a leader. If this safe environment is not in place, you will never be able to lead your team with a true coaching dynamic.

With the foundations of trust, growth mindset and psychological safety in place, you can then begin to introduce a team coaching culture. You will need to determine who in your team is ready for a coaching approach, based on their context, their experience and readiness. There will be team members who still require a more traditional leadership style from you (which is not automatically a reflection of their age). Your goal is to accommodate all your people and ignite all their potential. You cannot force coaching on someone if they just want to be managed.

Sharvani was a strong people-manager and had a reputation of supporting and nurturing her team. As part of her individual development plan, she identified that she needed to delegate more to her direct reports to free up time to take on new projects. This meant moving away from a traditional management style to more of an outcome-based approach where she would set her team goals and enable them to explore how best to achieve them. Through her assessment, she identified that of her five direct reports, three were ready for this shift and two would require further time and development. This meant that with the first three team members she was able to introduce a coaching approach and with the remaining two she continued for the short term with a more traditional management approach. This approach meant that she was able to delegate more, and she successfully delivered an additional project that year.

How to launch a coaching movement with your team

Establishing team purpose and norms

Does your team have a clear vision and purpose for the work that they are undertaking? What is the role that your team plays in helping achieve your organization's vision and purpose? Within this, how does the work integrate with people's own sense of purpose? As a leader coach, you can establish or co-create this mission with your team. This can be achieved collectively and cohesively by utilizing a coaching approach. How to do so will depend on the size and location of your team, for example this may need to be a virtual session if you have a remote team, and you may wish to have a facilitator so that you can fully contribute rather than simply lead. Your voice will matter, so depending on cultural nuances you will need to thoughtfully determine whether you speak first or last. Suffice to say, if your team believe you have come in with a ready-made answer you will lose the important opportunity to reach a solution through a coaching approach.

As part of this discussion the team can determine their norms – how they wish to work together and the agreed behaviours they will hold one another accountable for. This co-creation creates shared ownership so that it becomes a collective team responsibility, and you are accountable to maintain the guard rails. Ultimately, this will require the team to self-regulate on such matters rather than deferring automatically to the 'boss'. An important factor within this is conflict resolution; as a leader coach you will often encourage your team to resolve conflicts and find solutions rather than immediately deferring to you. However, it is important that you create some parameters around this as there will be areas where you need to intervene and give direction rather than coach.

Identifying opportunities to use a coaching approach

You will also need to define what operational success looks like and where collaboration is needed, and properly orchestrate the sharing of resources and deliverables so that the team works effectively together. You must communicate team goals and ensure these are cascaded down to the individual roles through your performance management system. As a leader coach you can then determine what can be a coaching opportunity and what needs greater direction from you. In my experience, there are only a few topics with limited potential for a coaching approach – these are mainly relating to areas such as compliance, governance, legal, fiscal and brand requirements. This means there will be many opportunities within your team's deliverables where the team members can be empowered by you to create new solutions and ways of working individually or collaboratively to deliver business outcomes.

This is an area where you need clarity and agreed parameters on your role. In most organizations, the manager sets goals, measures these and determines someone's performance rating or equivalent. When performance-related pay is part of the picture then the manager view is increasingly important. You will need to think early on about how you blend your existing role as a manager or leader and that of being a leader coach. Which version of you will be in the room, and how will you make this clear?

Over the course of the financial year, you will have a range of opportunities that will require different approaches, for example budget meetings, strategy sessions, update meetings, ideas generation and social gatherings. Set the parameters for each one, for example by arranging a simple, regular update session to ensure clear and consistent communication is in place across the team. This is of critical importance if you are working in a remote-working or hybrid model. Social gatherings can encourage non-work-related discussions so that people connect at a more personal level rather than simply by the roles they perform. Be clear about how your times together will be used and give clarity to your team as to what to expect and what is expected from them. This signposting is critical. The team need to clearly understand which perspective you are taking (manager, leader, leader coach, karaoke singer) and what you expect of them.

A framework to use with your team: GROW

A very useful tool to help introduce a coaching approach to your individual and team discussions is the GROW model developed by Sir John Whitmore.[11] We touched on this in Chapter 4 in relation to annual goal-setting with individual team members. Here, we explore its use in a team context to ensure the team has an opportunity to reflect on an issue, drive insight, explore options and agree collectively what the next steps and timings should be. Offering this approach to your team creates greater openness to build together and an opportunity for you to hone your team coaching skills. As the team builds trust and capability with this approach you can then begin to introduce more complex or contentious topics. As the leader coach you can facilitate the conversation and as the leader you can ensure that commitments made are subsequently owned and implemented.

Ashok had a challenge that he wanted to get his team to contribute on and decided to use the GROW model as a framework to engage everyone. The challenge he gave them to solve was how to reduce customer complaints on a specific service issue; he sent advance notice of the team coaching discussion, attached relevant materials to the invitation, and asked them to come prepared to speak up.

He started with the aim, which is reflected in the G of the model:

- **Goal** – what are you trying to achieve? The team agreed that they wanted to reduce complaints by 30 per cent in the next financial year.

Once this was established, he asked them to explore the R:

- **Reality** – where are you now? The team deliberated on the issue and identified the factors that were in their control and where there was support and collaboration from other functions in the business.

They then moved to O:

- **Options** – the options to close the gap between the Goal and Reality. It was here that creative thinking was unleashed as the team deliberated on several options to achieve the Goal. They ranked the options and voted to pilot the first three.

Finally, to agree to a way forward, Ashok focused on W:

- **Will** – what will you do? Here the team committed to working towards the goal, the deadline and determined who within the team would be responsible and accountable for which elements. They also let Ashok know they would need further resources from him in terms of headcount and maybe technology.

At this point in the meeting a plan was in place. Ashok indicated that he was shifting from coaching to a more directive approach. This was an important distinction for him to make so that the team had clarity about his intentions and expectations of them. He began assigning the required resources for the project and ensured that the deliverables became part of the performance management goal-setting for the year.

There are of course several different models you can use in coaching, I would encourage you to research, adopt and adapt what works for you and the people you are coaching. GROW is a good place to start with a team that is new to coaching, and there are plenty of alternatives you can add to your coaching toolkit.

Final thoughts

Evolving into the role of team leader as coach can be immensely rewarding. You can shape the environment in your team so that everyone can perform at their best and feel they belong. Thoughtfully applying your leader coach skills enables everyone to reach their potential, and this can be amplified even further when you create a coaching culture in your team. For many leader coaches, there is absolute joy and purpose in seeing your team soar through coaching.

This chapter wraps up Part 2 of this book, where our focus has been on bringing your coaching mindset and skills into your everyday role as a leader with individuals and teams. For the third and final part of the book, we look at how you can strengthen your organization's culture through formally coaching future leaders and paying attention to the wider organization system.

References

1 Leung, K, Bhagat, R S, Buchan, N R, Erez, M and Gibson, C B (2005) Culture and international business: Recent advances and their implications for future research, *Journal of International Business Studies*, 36 (4), 357–78

2 Hofstede, G (1983) The cultural relativity of organizational practices and theories, *Journal of International Business Studies*, 14 (2), 75–89

3 Hofstede, G (2001) *Culture's consequences: Comparing values, behaviors, institutions, and organizations across nations*, Sage Publications, Thousand Oaks, CA

4 Hofstede, G, Hofstede G J and Minkov, M (2010) *Cultures and Organizations: Software of the mind. Intercultural cooperation and its importance for survival*, 3rd edn, McGraw Hill, New York

5 House, R J, Dorfman, P W, Javidan, M, Hanges, P J and Sully de Luque, M (2013) *Strategic Leadership Across Cultures: The GLOBE Study of CEO leadership behavior and effectiveness in 24 countries*, Sage Publications, Thousand Oaks, CA

6 Pihlak, Ü and Alas, R (2012) Resistance to change in Indian, Chinese and Estonian organizations, *Journal of Indian Business Research*, 4 (4), 224–43

7 Meyer, E (2014) *The Culture Map: Breaking through the invisible boundaries of global business*, Public Affairs, New York

8 Dweck, C S (2006) *Mindset: The new psychology of success*, Random House, New York

9 Campbell, A (2019) *Effects of Growth and Fixed Mindset on Leaders' Behavior During Interpersonal Interactions*, Pepperdine: ProQuest Dissertations Publishing

10 Edmondson, A (1999) Psychological safety and learning behavior in work teams, *Administrative Science Quarterly*, 44 (2), 350–83

11 Mohapatra, C D (2016) Coaching for Performance by Sir John Whitmore, *NHRD Network Journal*, 9 (3), 68–70

PART THREE
Organizational lens
Having impact on the organization

Organization lens:
Having an impact on the
organization

Others lens:
Being a leader coach with
employees and teams

Self lens:
Focusing
on you as a
leader
coach

Formal coaching as a leader coach

8

LINDA BEATTY

As a leader coach your organization may offer the opportunity for you to provide formal coaching to colleagues to support their development. It's a fulfilling way to put your coaching skills into practice and can be incredibly rewarding. The following example is based on many leaders I have worked with.

> The feeling I get when I complete a coaching assignment with a colleague is utter elation, pride and satisfaction. To see how my own unique coaching style can have such a positive impact on someone is priceless. Coachees sometimes tell me at the first session that they feel their careers are going nowhere, they are unmotivated with no sense of purpose. After completing coaching sessions, they tell me they now have a clear vision and strategy. One coachee recently informed me that when they leave our coaching sessions, they believe they can achieve anything they set their mind to, and as a result they recently received a promotion. When one of my coachees nominated me for an internal recognition award 'enabling colleagues to thrive', I felt like I had succeeded. Knowing that my coachees can grow in confidence in their career due to a skill set that I helped them ignite is invaluable.

This chapter will help you prepare for formal coaching and consider how you can support your organization to help make it successful. We'll explore:

- preparing for formal coaching as a leader coach
- confidentiality and contracting
- managing boundaries
- coaching at different levels in the organization
- what organizations can do to make formal coaching successful

First, let's consider what formal coaching is and what the relationship would entail for you as a leader coach. Formal coaching is a structured coaching relationship between a skilled coach and an employee. While the coach can be internal or external to the organization, they should be outside of the employee's immediate work environment. The relationship is typically short-term where the coach and coachee agree to work together for a specific number of coaching sessions, usually 4–6, 60–90 minutes in duration, spread over a 3–12-month period. The focus for the coaching tends to be career or performance based allowing the coachee to set goals and work towards outcomes. This gives you the opportunity to practise your coaching skills in a more formalized way, while growing future leaders and being supported by your organization.

Preparing for formal coaching as a leader coach

Fully committing

From the outset it's important that you understand the time commitment this means for you as a leader coach. Many leader coaches are fulfilling their full-time role, in addition to formal coaching. Often, it's a good idea to agree a set time period so that you can fully commit and be present in your coaching sessions. Remember to include time to prepare for the sessions and for reflection. Also, it's important to decide how many colleagues you can coach at any one time to make sure you can fully commit to the coaching relationship.

Continuous development as a leader coach

Leader coaches combine their own personal development with their coaching practice, for example attending seminars and webinars, accessing supervision, and reading books and articles about coaching. It's important to have a holistic approach to your continuous development as a coach. Complementing coaching practice with personal development ensures that you remain in service to each coachee and bring the best of yourself to each session. Ongoing development as a leader coach has been covered in greater detail in Chapter 3.

Understand the coach/coachee matching process

You will need to build rapport with your coachee from the start of the relationship. Honesty, openness, authenticity and trust must be present from the initial conversations. This will help you and your coachee balance support and challenge in the relationship. Find out how the coach/coachee matching process works in your organization. Some organizations have a formal panel that determines matching, sometimes it's the responsibility of an individual who leads coaching, sometimes it's less formal, with coachees choosing a coach. Where matching is determined by someone else consideration will usually be given to leader coach capacity, geography, expertise or role level, etc. You might be asked to write a short biography introducing yourself as a coach. This is a good way for prospective coachees to learn what it might be like to work with you.

As an example, a coachee I recently spoke to suggested that they made their leader coach selection based on the bio, mainly due to the area of the business the coach worked in. The fact that the leader coach did not work in their division really appealed to them as they wanted complete reassurance regarding confidentiality. They were also drawn to the coach's personal interests, as this helped them understand the coach as a person.

Figure 8.1 A sample of what a leader coach biography might look like

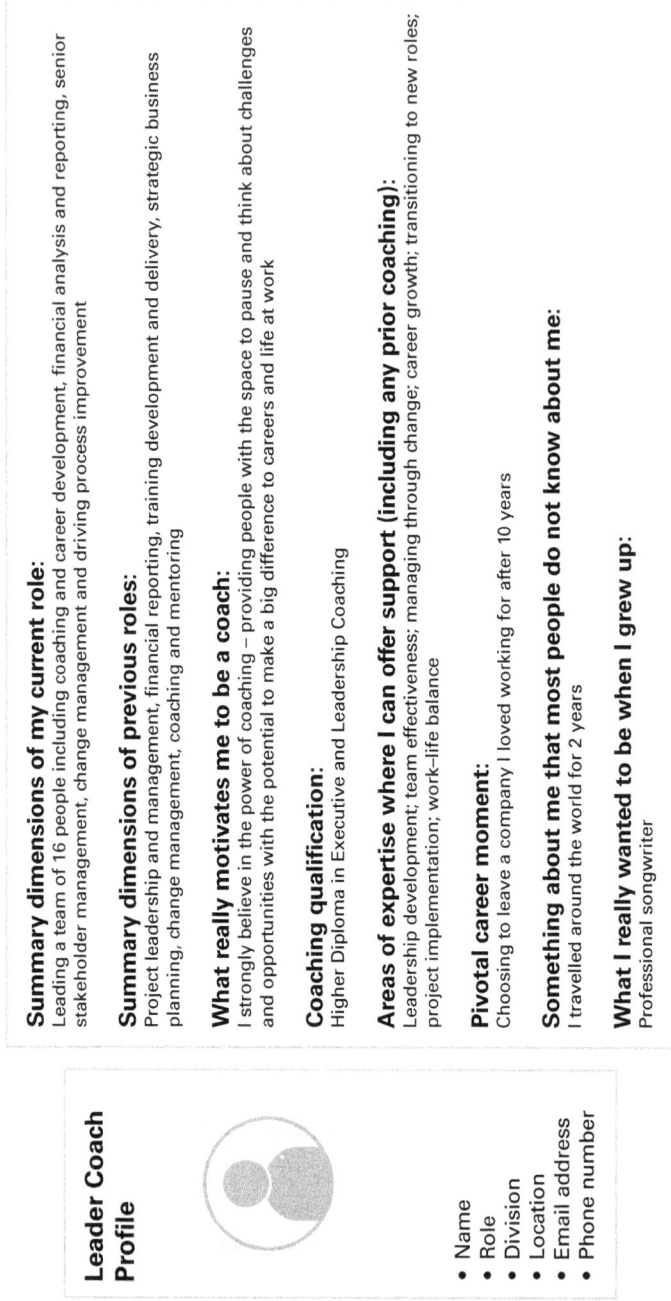

Leader Coach Profile

- Name
- Role
- Division
- Location
- Email address
- Phone number

Summary dimensions of my current role:
Leading a team of 16 people including coaching and career development, financial analysis and reporting, senior stakeholder management, change management and driving process improvement

Summary dimensions of previous roles:
Project leadership and management, financial reporting, training development and delivery, strategic business planning, change management, coaching and mentoring

What really motivates me to be a coach:
I strongly believe in the power of coaching – providing people with the space to pause and think about challenges and opportunities with the potential to make a big difference to careers and life at work

Coaching qualification:
Higher Diploma in Executive and Leadership Coaching

Areas of expertise where I can offer support (including any prior coaching):
Leadership development; team effectiveness; managing through change; career growth; transitioning to new roles; project implementation; work–life balance

Pivotal career moment:
Choosing to leave a company I loved working for after 10 years

Something about me that most people do not know about me:
I travelled around the world for 2 years

What I really wanted to be when I grew up:
Professional songwriter

If matching in your organization is based on coachees contacting you directly, there's a risk of being inundated with requests. This is where your commitment is important. Specifying how many colleagues you can work with at any one time gives you permission to say when you're at capacity. Equally you need to manage your ego and confidence if you are not approached by a coachee. These are normal emotions to address in either a support network group or supervision, explored more fully in Chapter 3.

Introduction to your coachee

Once matching is in place you should expect to get an overview or some description of the coachee. This might be done by the coachee's manager, or someone who sits more centrally such as an HR business partner, talent effectiveness manager, coaching lead or other coaching sponsor. How the overview is shared with you can vary. Let's explore a couple of scenarios.

Scenario 1

Your talent and effectiveness team has developed a new talent programme for female leaders. Only a select number of colleagues have been identified as candidates to attend. On attendance they are assigned an internal coach.

In this instance you should expect to get background on the programme, such as why was it developed, its content, objectives and expected outcomes. In addition, you should understand what's different about these colleagues and the reasons behind their selection. In this example, you may not get a profile of each individual coachee; rather a broad overview of the participant group.

Scenario 2

An HR business partner has identified a colleague in their area as high-performing talent. They feel that they would benefit from working with an internal leader coach to advance to the next stage of their career.

In this instance you should expect to get background on the person, the area of the business they are working in, challenges within the role, and what's known about their performance and approach. Their HR business partner is likely to provide you with an outline of the development gaps they feel could be addressed in coaching. While this overview is beneficial, it's not until you engage with this person that you both decide collectively what the area of focus for coaching will be.

Scenario 3

An employee is demonstrating low self-awareness around their behaviours, and their manager feels a coach could help them become more aware of the impact of their day-to-day actions.

As the leader coach, you would expect to get an overview of both the manager and the employee. You need a clear understanding of both the individuals and a broad overview of the conflicts or challenges. In this situation the manager is likely to have a clear idea of what the coaching should address (and may also benefit from coaching at some point). However, you would need to agree openly on the areas of focus with both the employee and manager. This type of coaching arrangement is considered a three-way partnership. I will discuss this more in the section below about contracting.

Regardless of how you are introduced to your prospective coachee, your first step will always be to arrange a chemistry meeting where you are both establishing if you would like to work together.

Confidentiality and contracting

Confidentiality

Confidentiality is key to the success of your coaching relationships and is vital for building trust.[1] As a leader coach you must never assume that confidentiality is implied, you must continuously acknowledge its presence. Reminding your coachee of this at every session is important, especially if you feel the coachee is holding something back.

> I recently spoke to a C-level executive who had been working with an external coach for over a year. They told me that they were holding back at their sessions as they were convinced the content of their discussions was being shared with their manager. I reminded them that confidentiality would restrict that from happening. To my surprise the executive had little memory of their initial contract or reassurance around confidentiality. My advice to them was to revisit the contract with their coach at the next session and re-contract around confidentiality.

This is an example of how a coachee will not be open if they feel dubious about confidentiality. It highlights the importance of constantly referring to the contract.

Contracting

It can be argued that a contract is the most important foundation for your coaching relationship.[2] It will govern your partnership right from the beginning and as you progress your contract will become a vital friend to both you and your coachee. Your contract can be written or verbal and should address several basic elements: confidentiality, logistics, ways of working and any other special conditions (e.g. three-way contract).

Confidentiality in contracting

One of the most important elements of your contract is confidentiality. It offers reassurance to your coachee that every conversation you have with them is bound by confidentiality, both now and in the future.

As a leader coach, you are likely to work with coachees unknown to you. This may not always be possible, but it is a privileged way to start your relationship as it is new and contains no bias. However, imagine having coached a colleague, and sometime later they are appointed to your team – they are now a direct report, or vice versa. How do you manage that relationship now? It's important that both of you still feel the comfort of your past contract and trust that confidentiality for past openness still exists.

Logistics

You will need to agree on logistics, including length, number, regularity of sessions and location (meeting room, virtual, outdoor, etc). Establish if your coachee would prefer virtual, on location or a blend of both if possible. Depending on the geography of your organization virtual may be the only option. If it is virtual, consider if your meeting will be by phone or video call. It's also important to acknowledge if the preference is to have the camera on or off. If it's in-person, you need to agree a meeting place. For example, is your coachee comfortable using a room in-house that has glass walls, or does it need to be more private? All these elements impact how you are going to connect with each other.

Ways of working

You will need to address ways of working or interacting with each other. For example, it's important for you to be able to challenge your client and provide constructive feedback. Your contract should establish permission for you to do this. That way your coachee will expect to be 'called out' and their thinking to be challenged in a non-threatening way. You should also build in a cancellation policy or expectations around cancellation. This is important so that coachees aren't tempted to cancel for unnecessary reasons, for example if they haven't completed their self-assigned 'homework' between coaching sessions.

Three-way contract

In Scenario 3, we explored the possibility of you entering a three-way coaching partnership with an employee and their manager. If you are invited to take part in this form of coaching, you will need to adapt your contract accordingly. In the case of a three-way partnership, there is likely to be a requirement for you to share issues arising in the coaching sessions with the manager. To ensure that the presence of feedback does not impact the trust between you and your coachee, you will need to clarify the process and structure for this feedback. Your contract must address what information is acceptable to share, by whom, and in what forum.

For example, one approach could be to allow time at the end of each session to recap and summarize the specific issue(s) the coachee feels are acceptable to share with their manager. Both you and your coachee would then meet with the manager, and the coachee would openly share the issue(s) with their manager in your presence. Your role would be to observe and facilitate this conversation, allowing each party equal portions of time to speak and subsequently agree an outcome. Permission to allow this scenario must be documented in the contract at the outset of coaching.

If it is a written contract, review and co-sign it with your coachee. This will extend to include the manager if you are establishing a three-way partnership. You are now ready to start coaching, using the contract at each session to reinforce what you have agreed.

Formal coaching framework

To summarize all that we have discussed so far in this chapter it might be helpful to visualize the process you could follow while providing formal coaching. To do this I have included a sample framework (Figure 8.2). It outlines the interaction between you and your coachee and your ongoing coaching development activities.

Managing boundaries

Managing boundaries is an aspect of your coaching practice that may create feelings of discomfort and internal conflict. This can happen when your commitment to confidentiality feels challenged by the information you discover about your coachee. To help you prepare for situations like this it's important to familiarize yourself with your organization's coaching policy regarding confidentiality so that you can maintain agreed boundaries. For example, a consultancy firm I'm familiar with has a policy that confidentiality will be upheld unless the coach believes the individual is at harm to themselves or others or is taking risks that could damage the firm. Consider what situation would need to be present for you to feel your boundaries are challenged. Here's an example of a leader coach, Ann, and her personal reflection on how she experienced a challenge to her boundaries.

Figure 8.2 Formal coaching framework

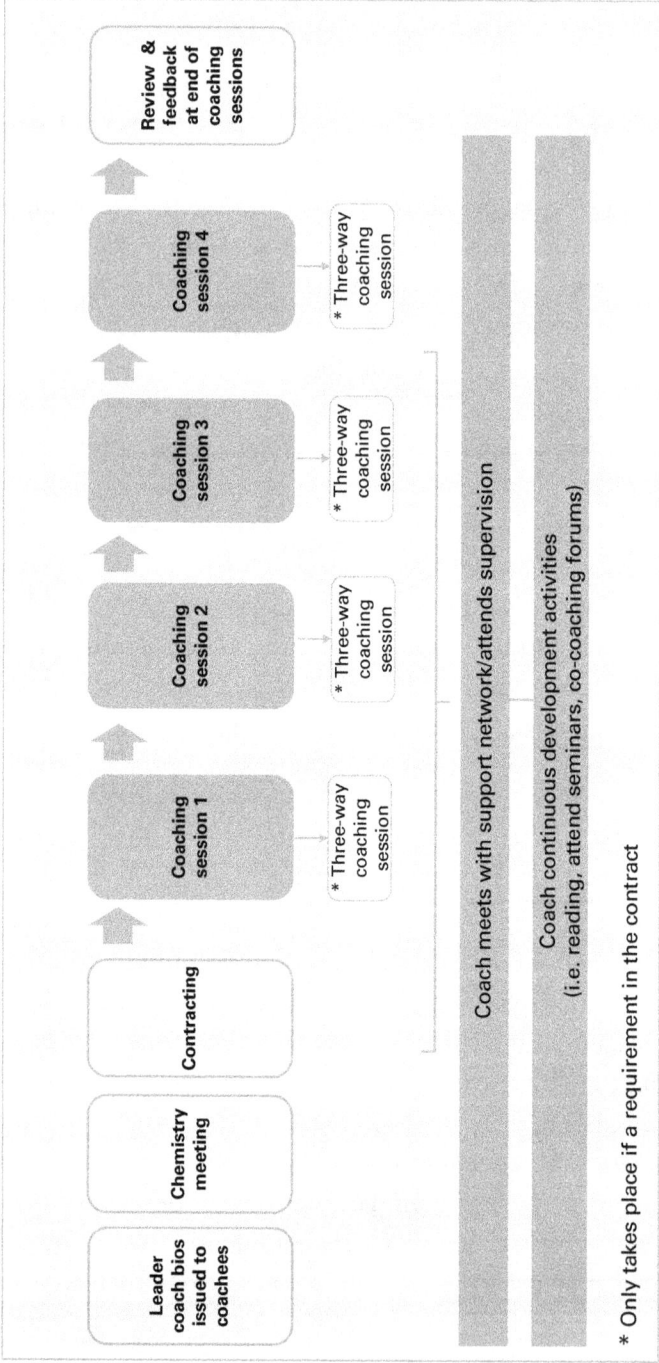

Leader coach bios issued to coachees

Chemistry meeting

Contracting

Coaching session 1 → * Three-way coaching session

Coaching session 2 → * Three-way coaching session

Coaching session 3 → * Three-way coaching session

Coaching session 4 → * Three-way coaching session

Review & feedback at end of coaching sessions

Coach meets with support network/attends supervision

Coach continuous development activities
(i.e. reading, attend seminars, co-coaching forums)

* Only takes place if a requirement in the contract

I underestimated the challenges that working as an 'internal' leader coach would present. My coachee was a middle-level manager in another part of the organization who was under significant pressure at work. She had very challenging expectations being made of her daily. It was apparent to me that she was not receiving support from her manager and that this was putting her under sustained stress and pressure.

Even though I had deliberately selected a coachee who worked in a different part of my organization I discovered that I knew some of the people that they worked with. I was aware of the challenges their department faced. Knowing the person my coachee wanted to discuss was very unhelpful, I felt conflicted. It was difficult for me to remain truly 'independent'. I was concerned for my coachee and was torn between respecting the confidentiality of the coach–coachee relationship and a desire to approach her manager.

Working with my coach supervisor and discussing the challenges I was facing in this coaching relationship ensured that I remained professional and ethical. The coaching supervision relationship helped me cope with the 'burden' I felt at that time.

Ultimately when you experience a situation that is challenging your boundaries, it is best practice to monitor how this is influencing your coaching relationship through your reflective practice and discuss in either your support network group or within supervision.[3]

Coaching at different levels in the organization

Regardless of whether an employee is a C-suite executive or an individual contributor, coaching benefits employees at all levels within an organization. It is more common to engage an external coach for C-suite executives, rather than an internal coach, unless there is someone within the organization with significant coaching experience and credibility. An external coach offers an external perspective and greater anonymity.

These components allow for trust to build within the relationship and in turn give the executive a space to show vulnerability. However, as an internal leader coach you have insights into your organization that an external coach does not. You understand your organization's political landscape along with its strategy, values and culture. Your unique perspective benefits coachees and because of this you can be a great coach to colleagues at all levels within your organization.

As discussed in Chapter 7, the wider cultural systems within which you coach can impact the perceived appropriateness of coaching people at different hierarchical levels. For example, if deference to hierarchy is strong it may be unacceptable for you to coach people more senior than you. In my experience as a leader coach, operating in an organization in western Europe, the question of role level has never arisen, but that may be different for you in your context. You will have to trust that meeting your coachee for the initial chemistry meeting will mutually guide whether or not you can agree to work together. It is important to acknowledge that you may have personal doubts or fears about coaching a colleague 'more senior' to you. If you are feeling this, ask yourself what this is really about for you. For example, is it a lack of confidence in your coaching? A belief you have about hierarchy? A sensitivity to power dynamics? The following example illustrates how a leader coach's experience of imposter syndrome nearly prevented them from agreeing to do something they knew they would personally benefit from.

Within my organization, I was asked to be part of a group of coaches providing formal coaching to coachees at a leadership level above my own. The sudden shift of excitement and enthusiasm was swiftly replaced by fear, and self-limiting beliefs flooded through me. I remember the overwhelming feelings: 'I can't do this'; 'what will these leaders think of me?'; 'what if the coachee feels the time they spend with me is unproductive?'; 'what if I am unable to coach?' I then looked for excuses to say no. 'I am too busy in my current role' or 'I don't have the capacity'. I then paused, took a step back and asked myself some honest questions. Why did I want to get involved in coaching? On reflection, I remembered all the time spent getting my accreditation, the positive feedback I gained from others I have coached (regardless of their level). I then had the confidence to begin mapping out what was possible and the steps I needed to take to accept this assignment.

A support network or coaching supervision session can help you explore any self-doubt you may be experiencing and deepen your insights about this to help you develop confidence. If you don't have access to support like this within your organization, you can seek support from a global coaching organization such as the Association for Coaching. The AC provides forums for coaches to connect and confidential group supervision experience calls for coaches to experience what supervision is like.[4]

Typical surface-level stories and deeper themes for coachees at different levels

Over the course of coaching sessions your coachee will typically share their story and reveal more of themselves. You will notice that within each narrative, 'surface-level' issues are disclosed, for example lack of promotion, loss of motivation, heavy workload, relationship challenges, communication differences, etc. As a leader coach when you unwrap those stories they translate into deeper themes; lack of confidence, self-doubt, fear, limiting beliefs, lack of presence, imposter syndrome, low self-awareness, lack of empathy and more. You will notice that stories and context from coachees at different levels may change but the underlying issues are often identical. Some of the typical surface-level stories you might hear from coachees at different levels in the organization and how these translate into similar issues at a deeper level are shown in Table 8.1.

Table 8.1 Typical stories and underlying themes addressed in coaching

Graduate

Colleague description	Surface-level story	Deeper theme
• First five years of career • Less understanding of own personal values • Seeking purposeful work • Needing feedback from manager • Keen to learn, seeking stretch challenges • Building skills • Starting to consider next role and career direction	• Thinking about skills they like/dislike using • Figuring out roles they like/dislike • Negotiating with direct manager • Learning how organizations work	• Self-awareness • Confidence • Beliefs • Presence • Doubt • Fear • Imposter syndrome

Team leader

Colleague description	Surface-level story	Deeper theme
• First people-management role • Supporting individuals other than themselves • Assessing workloads and outputs • Setting goals, holding reviews, giving feedback • Starting to think about their own personal values and career direction	• Worries about having direct reports • Dealing with various personalities • Managing stakeholders • Seeking their next promotion • Presenting/public speaking • Positioning themselves for their first people management role	• Self-awareness • Confidence • Beliefs • Presence • Doubt • Fear • Imposter syndrome

(continued)

Table 8.1 (Continued)

Experienced manager

Colleague description	Surface-level story	Deeper theme
• **Developing strategy** • **Goal setting/ reviews/giving feedback** • **Starting to understand their emotional intelligence and impact on their leadership style** • **Developing awareness of others and personality traits**	• Presence at meetings • Presenting/public speaking/storytelling • Learning how to say no • Seeking their next promotion • Managing peer stakeholders • Thinking about the next level and impact on their life	• Self-awareness • Confidence • Beliefs • Presence • Doubt • Fear • Imposter syndrome

Mid–senior-level manager

Colleague description	Surface-level story	Deeper theme
• **Strategist** • **Understanding the big picture** • **Gaining clarity on personal values and purpose** • **Leveraging their emotional intelligence strengths in leadership**	• Managing upwards • Dealing with difficult peer stakeholders • Working across the organization	• Self-awareness • Confidence • Beliefs • Presence • Doubt • Fear • Imposter syndrome

What organizations can do to make formal coaching successful

As a leader coach you play a part in the overall success of the coaching relationships and broader coaching-related initiatives. Notice what your organization is doing to make formal coaching a success and consider how you can support it. Some of the areas you might reflect on are:

- Organization culture: Are you noticing that coaching is becoming woven into the fabric of your organization's culture and values? Do you believe that the organization is bought into the impact and power of coaching? Are leaders and colleagues embracing a growth mindset by making and learning from mistakes?

- Role modelling: Who are the coaching role models within your organization? How do senior leaders promote and support coaching? Are they coaches, or do they engage in coaching in other ways?

- Support for coaching: Are you supported by your manager, by being 'freed up' to give time to your formal coaching practice? This will give you a sense of whether coaching is respected and valued. What is in place to support you to become a better coach, for example further coach training or access to forums to maintain your ongoing professional development? Are you encouraged to include the coaching you provide as part of your annual performance review?

- Goal setting: Most organizations will set out annual goals with their employees. Within your organization are these purely financially focused or are you encouraged to set personal development goals? Encouraging learning and development alongside achieving financial results is a sign that the organization is invested in developing a growth mindset.

All of this shows what your organization is doing to make coaching strategies and interventions successful. Chapter 9 will explore how coaching can be embedded at an organizational level to develop a coaching culture.

Organization coaching culture ecosystem

One of the ways in which an organization can make a success of formal coaching is by supporting the development of a coaching culture ecosystem. This contains components that support leader coaches and elevate coaching throughout the organization. Each component

Figure 8.3   Example of a coaching culture ecosystem

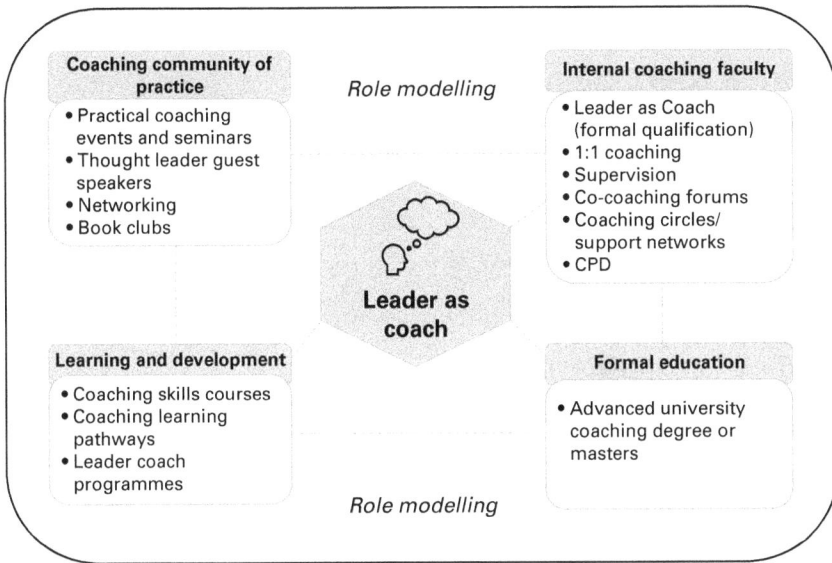

---

complements the others to nurture an organization's coaching environment and provides a range of support for leader coaches.

While it's unlikely to be your role to set up the entire coaching ecosystem, you can influence and support many of the components.

Coaching community of practice

Communities of practice (COP) are becoming more common in large organizations, where a group of colleagues with similar interests or qualifications come together.[5] The purpose of a coaching COP is to support the development of formally trained and self-taught coaches to create a coaching culture within the organization. It supports coaches to share skills and best practices, and provide feedback, through collaborative learning, professional development and networking. It tends to be colleague driven and grows organically, requiring members who are passionate about their expertise to activate the community. If you are a leader coach in a large organization, you could benefit from being a member of a group like this or could set one up yourself. If you are a leader coach in a smaller organization and would like to be part of a COP, look externally for support from coaching organizations such as the Association for Coaching.

Internal coaching faculty

Establishing an internal coaching faculty, by bringing together all the formally qualified coaches within the organization, is another way to embed coaching in your organization. Together, this group can collaborate on activities such as:

1 Providing individual coaching to each other.

2 Setting up support-networks to:

  (a) Facilitate co-coaching forums, allowing colleagues to practise their coaching skills in a safe environment, while receiving feedback.

  (b) Host coaching circles, where groups of coaches come together to peer supervise, share reading and practise coach models or tools.

3 Committing to regular coaching supervision.

4 Maintaining continuing professional development hours.

5 Adhering to a collective code of ethics.

This gives you an opportunity to meet and learn from other leader coaches in your organization. It's through this group that your support network, discussed in Chapter 3, is founded. If your organization is too small for this initiative, you can meet leader coaches in other organizations if you join a professional coaching body.

Learning and development

It's likely that as coaching becomes more embedded, colleagues who are not formally trained coaches will start to voice a desire to learn or know more about the practice of coaching. This appetite for learning can inform learning and development strategies, through activities such as coaching skills courses and leader as coach courses or pathways. These learning programmes empower colleagues to use coaching-style questions in everyday conversations while strengthening their listening skills.

Formal education

As colleagues become more interested in the craft of coaching, they develop a desire to study coaching in greater depth. The organization can support colleagues to gain external qualifications in coaching, such as certificates, diplomas or degrees.

The coaching ecosystem framework outlines initiatives that are complementary to each other and of equal importance. As a leader coach you can gain valuable growth through any such initiatives.

Final thoughts

Having read this chapter you should now have a good sense of what formal coaching looks like within an organizational setting and a clear understanding of what's required from you, should you decide to coach on a formal basis. Let's summarize the key points:

- Fully committing to coaching and having a continuous development plan are key to preparing to formally coach.
- It's important to be aware of the matching process within your organization and the different types of coachee introductions.
- Confidentiality should be never assumed; always address it, it is vital for the success of your coaching relationship.
- Spend time on your contract. Most challenges in coaching relationships come back to the coaching contract that was established.
- Expect to manage boundaries at some point, be aware of what action you need to take.
- Be open to coaching colleagues at different levels within your organization. Coachee stories may be different depending on their level; however, the underlying issues are notably similar.
- Consider the coaching ecosystem that exists in your organization. How can you support it?

I hope that as a leader coach you now feel better prepared, confident and excited to formally coach in your organization.

Finally, I would encourage you to re-read the story at the beginning of this chapter. Formal coaching provides an opportunity to shape people's lives, which is an incredible privilege.

References

1 Greenfield, D P and Hengen Jr, W K (2004) Confidentiality in coaching, *Consulting to Management*, 15 (1), 9–14
2 Hay, J (2007) *Reflective Practice and Supervision for Coaches*, Open University Press, Maidenhead
3 de Haan, E (2012) *Supervision in Action: A relational approach to coaching and consulting supervision*, Open University Press, Maidenhead
4 Association for Coaching (nd) Group supervision experience calls, www.associationforcoaching.com/page/EventsGroupSupervi (archived at https://perma.cc/MKM4-4QFV)
5 Wenger, E, McDermott, R and Snyder, W M (2002) *Cultivating Communities of Practice: A guide to managing knowledge*, Harvard Business School Press, Boston, MA

Strengthening organizational culture

9

JENNIFER KIDBY

You have an opportunity to influence the culture of your organization so that it's a healthier and more fulfilling workplace for future generations. It may sound bold, and it's true. Working alongside leader coaches within organizations, I have experienced the ripples that can be created when coaching is infused into everyday organizational life. This chapter will help you do this.

This is important work. I've seen, felt and heard the difference leader coaches make to colleagues who get to live in the culture that they created, the impact it has on their performance and how this filters through to their sense of self-worth. Leader coaches have told me that it's incredibly rewarding to have this sort of impact – to make an organization stronger than when you joined. Many have shared how personal it feels to them to be able to shape the workplace to be better for future generations. Just imagine, as a leader coach you have the skills, experience and mindset to create a place where human beings can thrive and achieve their potential. You can help build an organization where people feel heard, psychologically safe, challenged, and supported to do their best work. You get to author a page in the experience your organization creates for its employees. That's an incredible opportunity. You might not feel that as one individual you can make a difference. You can. You are a role model for your team – we learn to lead from the people who lead us.

One senior leader I worked with said that it wasn't until they had been in their new senior leadership role for a few months that they began to see the opportunity they had. Not just to coach and develop future leaders, but to shape the culture of their organization.

In this chapter we'll first explore the global trends that are shaping the context for organizations and the changing shape of the workforce. This is the backdrop for your opportunity as a leader coach. We'll then look at how organizations are responding, including the journey that many are making towards a coaching culture. The focus will then shift to you as a leader coach; how to evolve how you think about your organization and what to put in place to have impact at an organizational scale. We'll close this chapter by considering some of the challenges you may experience and how you can create support mechanisms for yourself.

The wider context for organizations

Let's start by looking at the wider context for organizations and what this means for you as a leader coach. You may have heard of the term VUCA; volatile, uncertain, complex and ambiguous. It was originally used in the military and has been used frequently since the late 1980s to describe the sort of world we live in. It has been useful to inspire and provoke leaders and organizations to be responsive and flexible in a rapidly changing world. It's still frequently used and yet somehow seems an inadequate way to capture the essence of what's happening around us. The multiple crises facing the world are felt every day in organizations (such as the climate crisis, global power dynamics, pandemics, social inequality, systemic racism and economic instability). The world is changing, fast, through crises like these and longer-term changes that will have a transformational impact on society, such as scarcity of resources, demographic change, generational differences, and digital and technological shifts. This impacts the decisions that leaders need to make and shapes the expectations of younger and often more vocal generations. The increasing frequency, interconnection and cumulative impacts demand new ways to describe the world we're in to help us make sense of it and choose how to respond.

A 'beyond VUCA' mindset I've found to be useful is the BANI framework from author, anthropologist and futurist, Jamais Cascio.[1] Cascio states that our world is Brittle, Anxious, Non-linear and Incomprehensible:

- **Brittle** – attempts to maximize efficiency have led to a world where there is no room for error or change. Any small weakness or unexpected change leads to collapse. We no longer have excess capacity for the unexpected.

- **Anxious** – a fear that uncertainty has reached a point where any choice we make may be the wrong one, fuelled by social media and the threat of shame. This can paralyse us as leaders and our organizations.

- **Non-linear** – cause and effect are so far apart and often seemingly unconnected. It seems impossible to predict consequences.

- **Incomprehensible** – extreme complexity means that attempting to find all the answers is impossible. There's so much noise and data overload that it's unrealistic to imagine we can understand everything. Old leadership habits, which worked in a more predictable world, often lead us to gather more data, which leads to even greater overwhelm. Enough is never enough.

At first glance it might be disheartening to think about life in a BANI world. It's essential that organizations respond to the way the world is unfolding; it's the only way they will survive and it's essential if they are going to thrive. However, there is good news, as a leader coach you already have skills that will help you and your organization:

- Collaboration, strong teams and clear communication will soften **brittleness**.

- Empathy, awareness and mindfulness will help cope with **anxiety**.

- Openness, perspective taking and adaptability will help people work with **non-linearity**.

- Transparency and trust in intuition will help make decisions in an **incomprehensible** world.

Sound familiar? These are all qualities of a leader coach that you are likely developing already. When you allow coaching to infuse through everything you do you create an environment that strengthens your organization to survive and even thrive in a BANI world.

Changing shape of the workforce

The shape of workforces continues to evolve.[2] There is increased diversity from multiple generations, ethnicity, neurodiversity, physical diversity, gender identity, sexual orientation and more. This brings opportunities to create an inclusive environment where people feel they belong and are safe to bring their whole selves to work. I've worked in organizations where leader coaches have done this, and the impact is incredible. Colleagues are willing to bring different perspectives, put new ideas on the table, support each others' growth, speak highly of their employer to potential employees and customers, celebrate success, be willing to learn, embrace change and bring joy into their working lives. It takes focused and aligned effort to create a culture like this, it won't happen by accident. You can start by thinking about the rich diversity that your organization already has and how this will grow in the coming years. What can you do to make it even more diverse? What sort of environment can you create to encourage employees from a wide range of backgrounds and different life experiences to share their perspectives? For example, in 2020, 70 per cent of organizations reported that leading multigenerational workforces was important to short-term success, but just 10 per cent were very ready to address this.[3]

I hosted a dinner conversation with leaders to explore the challenges and opportunities they had from leading a workforce with at least four different generations and where expectations of work were shifting. There were a range of opinions around the table. Some felt that those joining the workforce needed to be more grateful for the opportunities they had, some said older generations needed to change with the times, and one or two voices expressed a view that there were far more opportunities than challenges. They believed the key to unlocking potential for the business was to listen, ask great questions and be open to different perspectives.

Our workforces are becoming more diverse and this brings a massive opportunity to unlock potential. When employees feel a sense of inclusion, equity and belonging, they are more likely to feel engaged and committed to the organization. And this starts with the environment that is created through systems and processes in the organization as well as how individual leaders behave. As a leader coach you have core coaching skills that will help you do this, including listening, questioning, perspective taking, empathy and creating a safe space for people. How to do this as a team leader is explored further in Chapter 7.

The changing role of work in people's lives is also impacting organizations. This was accelerated by the Covid-19 pandemic where the disruption and distress many people experienced led them to re-evaluate what was important in life.[4] World Economic Forum data from 2022 showed work–life balance, flexibility and mental health were topping the list of what people considered most important.[5] A wider variety of employment patterns emerged in workplaces in response, such as part-time working arrangements, flexible schedules, job shares, hybrid working, gigs, temporary contracts and 'work from anywhere' policies. A blend of in-person and virtual working became more common and brought greater flexibility for employees to find work–life balance. It also presented a challenge; how to strengthen engagement and connection when employees are less frequently together in person and boundaries can become blurred.

The changing context for organizations brings challenges and many opportunities. The BANI-ness of our world, the increasing complexity of our workforces, and the changing role that work plays means that organizations need to respond to be sustainable and successful. Let's look more at how organizations are responding and where your leader coach mindset and skills can have a significant impact.

How organizations are responding

Organizations have traditionally been built on the underlying assumption that the world is complex but can be understood. This was a sound response to a world that was more predictable and where success could be found from fast innovation and increased efficiency. Humans could be seen as predictable resources, control held by a few people at senior levels, and ongoing exponential growth seen as a realistic and healthy goal. As you know, that's not the world we live in today. There is a need for something different, for an organizational model that is less mechanistic, more adaptable and more humanistic than before. Some organizations have started to experiment with this. Even before the pandemic, organizations were implementing different ways of organizing, distributing power and making decisions. For example, Frederic Laloux's thought-provoking work in his book *Reinventing Organizations* paints a picture of organizations evolving around three core themes – self-management, wholeness and evolutionary purpose.[6] These are organizations where people are seen as more than parts of a machine. There is greater empowerment, less hierarchy, a wider range of stakeholders and an environment that encourages people to bring their whole self to work.

Coaching is at the heart of organizations like this because it is essential to engage and unlock potential of a diverse workforce. The old command-and-control approach doesn't work, especially in an unpredictable world where no one has all the answers. The insights and experiences of everyone are needed, and this can only happen where people feel they belong and are valued for their perspectives and contribution. Organizational culture becomes a strategic driver of success, often with coaching at its heart. Leader coaches like you are essential because you have the skills and mindset to bring a coaching culture to life.

A coaching culture

So, what is a coaching culture? At a surface level a coaching culture could be considered to exist when leaders and managers develop coaching skills and are encouraged to have coaching conversations. Is this enough for a coaching culture to take root? In my experience it's an important tactic but not sufficient if you want coaching to truly be built into the culture and DNA of an organization. A strong coaching culture embeds the essence of a good coaching relationship in how the organization operates; where relationships are built on trust and openness, feedback is frequently given and sought, and curiosity is valued and encouraged. Processes and systems, such as recruitment, performance management and leadership succession, are shaped by a coaching mindset. There is a focus on broader professional and personal development, not just technical expertise. Senior leaders consistently let go of power and delegate control to employees so that the organization benefits from the potential of everyone. There's an acceptance that it's OK if everything isn't 100 per cent perfect and that failure is sometimes necessary for people to develop and grow. Overall, an environment is created where employees feel valued, are more engaged and feel a part of something bigger than themselves. It becomes a place to thrive as a human being.

Getting there is an ongoing journey that needs consistent action and reinforcement from leaders like you. Some organizations have struggled to create a coaching culture because of inconsistency and misalignment – where leaders say the right words but aren't consistent in their actions or don't build systems in the organization that support a coaching culture. This leads to cynicism and disengagement – 'I told you so' becomes the cry from employees who dared to hope that something was changing and then felt their hopes dashed. This weakens trust and engagement, which in turn negatively impacts performance.

You're reading this book so it's likely your organization has started this journey, or you might be interested in how you can ignite interest in coaching. Table 9.1 will help you to gauge where your organization is at and what you can do to build momentum and strengthen culture.

Table 9.1   Different stages of a coaching culture

	Early stage of the journey	Coaching is well established	Coaching culture is a part of the DNA
What this stage can look like in your organization	Focus is on developing technical expertise, short-term results and goals	Same as earlier stage, plus a focus on values and the unique contribution someone can make to achieve longer-term outcomes	Same as earlier stages, plus a focus on individual and organizational purpose, and growth as a human being
Tensions you might experience as a leader coach	Seeing employees working within organizational systems that encourage them to focus on short-term financial measures at the expense of broader outcomes	Balancing how to empower employees when you are still accountable for results	Seeing that people may need to leave the organization to truly live their purpose and grow
How you can build momentum and strengthen culture	Share stories that show where coaching has had a positive impact on short- and long-term outcomes	Let go of control and enable employees to take ownership for outcomes. Act on opportunities to build coaching into how the organization operates	Show vulnerability in sharing how purpose shows up in work and life

Having visible support – in words and actions – from senior leaders is essential to build a coaching culture. I'm often asked how to get senior leaders to buy in to coaching, for example how to convince leaders to invest time to participate in coach training and then to coach their employees. This question is usually a sign that an organization is at an early stage of the journey, where coaching is seen as a tactic rather than at the heart of culture and way of being. What's needed is role modelling from senior leaders and a clearer alignment between coaching and business outcomes. Once this is in place momentum often builds with more leaders and managers requesting coaching skills training and more employees wanting coaching. These two things – alignment and role modelling – are essential foundations. Without them it will be a struggle to establish a coaching culture.

What you can do as a leader coach

There's a lot you can do to strengthen your organization's culture. Your leader coach training will have helped you develop skills in taking different perspectives, questioning assumptions and shifting thinking. You can use these skills to help your colleagues and organization respond to the world we're living in, and maybe even shape the future.

Transactional to transformational thinking

Traditional and transactional ways of thinking about organizations can lead you to see cause and effect as a linear relationship, one where the future can be predicted from the past. When things changed more slowly in the world and there were fewer interconnections, you could rely on your experience (and others' experiences) to predict what would happen next and how you should respond. A more traditional and transactional way of thinking was useful. With the unpredictability we now live with, the older thinking patterns that helped you control, predict and plan no longer seem up to the job. A more transformational and interconnected way of thinking is needed. Table 9.2 shows what this can look like.

Table 9.2 Shifting from a transactional to transformational way of thinking

From transactional	To transformational
Take one perspective	Seek multiple perspectives
Focus on the individual parts of the organization	Focus on the relationships between the parts
Either/or thinking	Both/and thinking
Get stuck in seeking certainty before making decisions	Become OK with good enough decisions
Believe you have the 'right' answers already	Be curious and enquire into what others think

Let's bring this to life with some examples. Think about your organization or one you know well, and what it is doing in the space of diversity, equity, inclusion and belonging and what it is doing to embed a coaching culture.

Example 1: Diversity, equity, inclusion and belonging

An organization taking a transactional approach might have a leader or team running many discrete initiatives such as external speaker events, employee resource groups for different groups of employees, and marketing/social media posts and campaigns. It might be tracking data about the numbers of people being recruited in different groups. These are all useful initiatives; however, an organization taking a more transformational approach would go further. It would look at how diversity, equity, inclusion and belonging can be woven throughout its culture and processes, embedding it into leadership development, succession planning, engagement strategies and communications. Consideration would be given to intersectionality and understanding the interconnected nature of social categorizations as they apply to an individual or group of employees. Data would be gathered to show paths of different groups through the organization, for example looking at turnover and tenure at different role levels, and movement through the organization. Stories would be shared that invite compassion and enquiry into employee experiences. It's not that the transactional approach is bad or should not be undertaken, but that the transformational way of thinking and acting is necessary for broader impact and to make progress.

Example 2: Coaching culture

Another example is coaching. How is coaching embedded in your organization's culture? A transactional approach might include mandatory coach training for managers where they are encouraged to develop and use skills in their conversations with their teams. A transformational approach would be signalled by role modelling from the most senior leaders who frequently share stories about their own growth, development and vulnerability. They openly bring their whole selves into how they show up at work. All employees are encouraged to develop coaching skills, which are seen as core business skills rather being talked about as optional or 'soft' skills. Leaders continue their coach development journey through activities like masterclasses, co-coaching, supervision and skills development. (You can read more about ongoing professional development as a leader coach in Chapter 3.) You might also find coaching institutionalized through processes such as formal feedback mechanisms, promotion criteria and performance management. Again, a transactional approach will get you so far, but a transformational strategy has more tentacles into the whole organization.

Example 3: You as a leader coach

You can also apply a transactional and transformational lens to how you bring coaching into your work and life. A transactional approach might mean that you have a coach mode – a time and place where you are using coaching skills, maybe in formal coaching sessions or in regular check-ins with your team. It's something you switch on in these situations. A transformational approach would mean you are bringing coaching into all aspects of your leadership, at work and beyond. It's the difference between 'doing' coaching and integrating coaching mindset and skill into your whole life; how you are 'being' as a leader coach.

Many leaders have discovered that coaching is so much more than a set of skills to use with colleagues. Experiencing the emotional depth of relationships that coaching can create has been transformational for many leaders at an incredibly personal level. They progress through their coach development journey having changed how they show up with colleagues and in their wider relationships outside of work, particularly as a partner, parent or friend.

Keep in mind that transformational isn't better than transactional, or vice versa. Both are important and valuable in the right context. What's important is that there is alignment with the environment. A transactional response is highly effective in an industry or market that is predictable, where what worked last year is likely to work again this year. There's no need to encourage different ways of thinking as you already know what you need to do to be successful. However, a transformational way of being is a more useful response to a world that is continuously shifting, and at a faster and more unpredictable pace each year. Think back to the BANI world described earlier in this chapter; in this environment it's impossible to predict the future. Your leadership needs to draw out the very best thinking and broadest perspectives from people, which means you need an engaged team who are willing to share their experiences and ideas. A coaching culture is the key to creating this environment.

Tools to develop transformational thinking

Transformational thinking is a skill you can develop in yourself and your team/colleagues to improve the quality of thinking in your organization. Two tools that can help you do this are explained below. If you want to develop your toolkit further, I recommend looking at the work of Richard Boston and Karen Ellis in their book *Upgrade: Building your capacity for complexity* and Jennifer Garvey Berger's book *Unlocking Leadership Mindtraps*.[7,8] Both will equip you to transform the way you think.

1 **Develop transformational thinking skills.** Deliberately think from the perspective of multiple stakeholders. List the different

stakeholders impacted by your decisions. Make your list as broad as you can. This could include:

o your team

o different departments or teams in your organization

o clients/customers

o shareholders

o local community

o the environment/climate

o future generations

Walk in the shoes of each stakeholder group. From their perspective, write down what they need from you. What do they want you to be thinking about? Now apply this thinking to your decisions. This is a useful team activity for when you want your team to think differently about the impact they have.

2 **Practise paradoxical thinking**. Hold seemingly opposing ideas in your mind at the same time as you work through a challenge or decision. This will bring greater creativity and flexibility in your thinking patterns. It's another powerful tool to use with a team. To identify the paradoxes in your organization, think about where there are tensions or perceived contradictions. Those frequently mentioned by leader coaches include:

o Operational – Strategic

o My team/division/department – Whole organization

o Purpose – Profit

o Empower others – Be accountable for results

Now think about a decision you need to make. Consider what you would do if you focused on just one end of each paradox. Now think about what possibilities exist if you address both ends of the paradox. This might lead you to a different solution. Even if it doesn't it begins to expand your thinking and train your mind to think paradoxically.

Strengthening culture

A more transformational mindset in an organization creates a stronger foundation for strategies that will strengthen the culture. As a leader coach your role might give you a platform to influence organization-wide systems and processes. Look for opportunities to have impact at scale and beyond your individual relationships – what can be put in place that will institutionalize what's most important to your organization's culture? Some things I've seen that have an impact at scale are shown in Table 9.3.

Table 9.3   How to strengthen culture at scale

Strengthening culture at scale	Potential impact
Recruit and build a team that represents the broadest diversity of thinking and experience.	Increases diversity in thinking and openness to different perspectives. No one has the whole picture by themselves. Once you have a more diverse team, make sure you actively encourage different ideas and perspectives to be shared.
Develop coaching skills at all levels in the organization.	Develops coaching skills in all managers and shows them how to use them in their everyday role. Also help them to gain clarity on when coaching is not a useful approach. Not every conversation has to be a coaching conversation.
Build coaching into how performance is assessed and rewarded.	Demonstrates that the organization values coaching, for example by making coach training and ongoing practice part of promotion requirements.
Establish two-way mentoring – across the organization if you can; if not, then do it in your team and share what you're doing with other leaders.	Strengthens openness, trust and belonging, and signals a different approach from a more typical hierarchical top-down mentoring strategy. It has greatest impact when you match employees who can learn from each other, for example senior leaders can share organizational knowledge and experience with younger employees who can provide mentoring on their lived experience working in the organization at a different level in the hierarchy.

(continued)

Table 9.3   (Continued)

Strengthening culture at scale	Potential impact
Create a shadow board to advise the senior team.	Brings different perspectives to decision making from a different level in the organization. It also creates a leadership development opportunity for more junior colleagues.
Create platforms to share stories that illustrate the culture the organization is striving towards. Glimpses of the future can be found in the present.	Puts a spotlight on the things you want to see more of. For example, use internal communication channels for senior leaders to talk publicly about how they make flexibility work for them. Hearing a leader say they are taking two hours off in the middle of the day to do something important in their wider life is powerful. Whether it's going to their kid's school event, getting a massage, or taking the car to the garage, it's showing that flexibility is OK and encouraged here. It's one way to develop a high-performance culture based on trust.
Role model visibly and vocally so your team can see you mean it. Show, don't tell.	Be a role model by doing the things you want to see more of. Actions speak louder than words. If you want a high-performance culture where people have rich and varied lives and are trusted to get the work done, show them that you do this in your own life. Be the person who sits on the board of a local charity, or volunteers at the local food bank, or openly shares the skills they're developing, including mistakes along the way. Celebrate successes in your team.
Collaborate with people with different perspectives on the things that are most important to the organization.	Encourages broader thinking, collaboration, dialogue. It also shows that healthy disagreement is valued and can be respectful.

(continued)

Table 9.3 (Continued)

Strengthening culture at scale	Potential impact
Deliberately use language that aligns with the culture you want.	Chapter 5 explores language as a leader coach. Challenge the use of culturally misaligned language wherever you can. You're painting pictures in people's minds, and that can evoke an emotional response. Use the language that aligns with the culture.
Always role model curiosity, deep listening and being present as essential leadership practices.	As you take on more senior roles, what you say and do (and what you don't) is amplified whether you like it or not. More people will watch you and take their cues from you.

If your role doesn't yet lend itself to having an organization-wide impact, there will still be opportunities to influence and experiment on a smaller scale. Think about your team or department. You can have an impact through your individual relationships. Think about the stories you can share, tools you can use and language you can reinforce. You can encourage your team to use coaching behaviours both when working together as a team, and as individual leaders. You can read more about how to do this in Chapter 7. Every interaction is an opportunity to reinforce and strengthen culture.

Developing future leaders

Another powerful way you can strengthen your organization's culture is by developing future leaders in your team. Leaders emerge from being in environments where their current ways of thinking and being are no longer sufficient. This demands a change in mindset and develops different skills. Nick Petrie, who specializes in leadership development and formerly worked at the Center for Creative Leadership, says that you can create these conditions for people in your team through creating stretching experiences, exposing them to different perspectives, and help them make meaning.[9] This framework was explored in Chapter 3 in relation to your development as a leader coach; here's how you can use it to guide and support others' development and growth:

1 **Stretch experiences:** create stretching experiences that will stretch colleagues outside their comfort zone. Help them find opportunities to have an impact on a larger scale or scope within the organization. For example, if someone has always had accountability for results at a team or department level put them in a situation where their impact is wider, such as an organization-wide task force or strategic project. This experience will be a catalyst for them to find new ways of thinking and working.

2 **Colliding perspectives:** work with different perspectives. Identify assignments where colleagues must work with different people to successfully achieve their goals. This could be working with colleagues from a different department with different technical expertise, from outside the organization, or at a different role level within the organizational structure. This will develop perspective-taking and empathy.

3 **Elevated sense-making:** make meaning. Having new experiences and stretching assignments require reflection to draw out the learning so that it is replicable in future situations. You can do this by asking questions to help colleagues think more deeply about their experiences through regular check-ins. Another option is to have them work with a coach who is skilled at helping leaders shift their mindset.

These three things combined will help accelerate the development of future leaders who can strengthen your organization's culture. They will expand the way they think, be more open to different perspectives and be invested in their own development and growth. They will be better prepared for future leadership roles and challenges that will face organizations in an increasingly unpredictable world. It's a way for you to leave a legacy as a leader coach.

Finding your courage when you feel alone

You might find that the mindset and skills you are developing align well with your organization's culture – where curiosity, collaboration and growth mindset are encouraged. It might even be a part of how your performance is assessed. If this sounds familiar, congratulations! You are in an environment where you're likely to be nudged to put what you have learnt into practice. Leader coaches in organizations where coaching is seen as a core part of the DNA feel they are supported in using what they've learnt because there is strategic and cultural alignment.

When the culture doesn't yet encourage coaching

You'll already know that not every organization is like this and for some leader coaches it's a very different story. They feel like a lone voice in a culture where coaching isn't valued or is seen as a 'nice to have' only when things are going well. This can also happen in organizations whose espoused culture and actual culture don't align. What is said by senior leaders and the daily lived experience of employees is very different. It can feel demoralizing, knowing the impact that a coaching culture can have and being in an environment where it isn't valued. If this sounds like your organization, you can still put into practice what you've learnt on a smaller scale. Look again at the tactics earlier in this chapter. Maybe there are some that you can implement at a local level with your team or a small number of employees. Experimenting at the edges of an organization can sometimes produce results that begin to ripple into the mainstream.

Finding the right pace

Sometimes leader coaches are passionate and inspired to transform every conversation they have, and at a pace that is too fast for the organization's culture. This can feel empowering, even revolutionary, but comes with a risk of being too different, too fast. I've seen this happen several times in different organizations. A coaching programme is introduced, often at entry or middle-manager level, and managers complete the programme feeling full of optimism and passion for putting their new coaching skills into practice. They then leap into every conversation with deep questions or enquiring into someone's deeper emotions without having established permission. I've heard this referred to in a derogatory fashion as being too coachy-coachy, an overuse of a coaching style that felt inappropriate, poorly timed and at worst, intrusive. While it usually comes with good intentions, it can turn colleagues against coaching. It's important to remember not every conversation needs to be a coaching conversation.

A C-suite leader was a strong supporter of coaching, and yet was also critical of some colleagues who seemed to want to turn every conversation into a coaching one. He felt the questions they would ask seemed too personal, too soon, without trust having been developed. There was a level of permission that hadn't been agreed, and he often felt conflicted between wanting to support the company's shift towards a coaching culture and wanting to maintain his personal boundaries.

This is where permission for the type of conversation you want to have becomes very important. Dr David Rock, Director of the NeuroLeadership Institute, says that it's important to check in with people and ask permission to have a conversation that potentially goes deeper or is more personal or sensitive than usual.[10] This creates openness and helps the person be ready for the conversation. For example, if you wanted to have a conversation with someone about missing deadlines you might say something like 'I've noticed recently that you haven't been hitting some key milestones and I'd like to understand more about what's been going on for you. Is now a good time to explore this, or shall we meet tomorrow?' This gives clarity about what you want to discuss, and respects that now might not be a good time. It pre-frames the conversation you're going to have, which helps the person to be in the right mindset.

Finding support

It can be discouraging when you don't see the culture shifting as far and fast as you think it needs to. It's easy to feel that your efforts aren't having the impact you want. In these moments have people around you who can cheer you on. This could be other leader coaches who have been through similar training in your organization and can relate to the challenges you are navigating, other professionals in your organization who are passionate about evolving the culture, or experienced coaches. It can also be useful to connect with a professional coaching organization such as the Association for Coaching that offers ongoing development for leader coaches and a global coaching community.

Final thoughts: A sense of hope

In this chapter we've looked at how organizations are evolving in response to the world around us, and the shifts and changes in the workforce leading to greater flexibility and a more human workplace. The skills and mindset you have as a leader coach can play a vital role. In closing this chapter I'd like to share with you the sense of hope I have from having worked with many leader coaches in different organizations and industries. Sometimes it can take weeks, months or years to see the impact you've had on an organization. Keep going. I've been inspired by many who are on this journey to keep learning and growing so that they can strengthen culture and create a place where everyone can contribute and feel they belong.

References

1 Cascio, J (2020) Facing the age of chaos, Medium, 29 April, www.medium.com/@cascio/facing-the-age-of-chaos-b00687b1f51d (archived at https://perma.cc/CPG8-MN53)

2 Belelieu, A and Nazeri, H (2020) How a multi-generational workforce is key to economic growth, World Economic Forum, 16 December, www.weforum.org/agenda/2020/12/how-a-multi-generational-workplace-is-key-to-economic-growth/ (archived at https://perma.cc/67CJ-TFVH)

3 Schwartz, J et al (2020)The postgenerational workforce: From
    millennials to perennials, Deloitte Insights, 15 May, www2.deloitte.
    com/us/en/insights/focus/human-capital-trends/2020/leading-a-multi-
    generational-workforce.html (archived at https://perma.cc/8GHX-
    NV6H)

4 Alexander, A, De Smet, A, Langstaff, M and Ravid, D (2021) What
    employees are saying about the future of remote work, McKinsey &
    Company, 1 April, www.mckinsey.com/capabilities/people-and-
    organizational-performance/our-insights/what-employees-are-saying-
    about-the-future-of-remote-work (archived at https://perma.cc/
    QCK5-GXHR)

5 Wood, J (2022) What do employees want most from their work life in
    2022?, World Economic Forum, 21 February, www.weforum.org/
    agenda/2022/02/what-do-employees-want-most-from-their-work-
    life-in-2022/ (archived at https://perma.cc/2HT6-8S8M)

6 Laloux, F (2014) *Reinventing Organizations: A guide to creating
    organizations inspired by the next stage in human consciousness*,
    Nelson Parker, Belgium

7 Boston, R and Ellis, K (2019) *Upgrade: Building your capacity for
    complexity*, LeaderSpace, London

8 Garvey Berger, J (2019) *Unlocking Leadership Mindtraps: How to
    thrive in complexity*, Stanford University Press, Stanford, CA

9 Petrie, N (2018) The How-To of Vertical Leadership Development – Part
    2: 30 Experts, 3 Conditions, and 15 Approaches, White Paper, Center
    for Creative Leadership, https://14226776-c20f-46a2-bcd6-5cefe57153f.
    filesusr.com/ugd/a8b141_7243e9c83c01457eac15f6cd69073de2.pdf
    (archived at https://perma.cc/MKF5-3TZV)

10 Rock, D (2007) *Quiet Leadership: Six steps to transforming
    performance at work*, HarperCollins Publishers, New York

Final thoughts: The power and potential of a leader coach

JENNIFER KIDBY

The impact that coaching mindset and behaviour has can be transformative. Throughout this book you've read about how to develop yourself as a leader coach, bring coaching into your everyday leadership role with others and strengthen a coaching culture in your wider organization. These three lenses are useful to keep in mind: self, others and organization.

As you explored in the first part of this book, the 'self' lens, being a leader coach means understanding how your beliefs and habits shape your behaviour. This is particularly powerful when it comes to the beliefs you may have about the value you bring as a leader coach. Many leader coaches experience a shift in identity; from feeling their value is rooted in having the right answers and technical expertise towards seeing their value in developing others and growing future leaders. You might discover that the growth you experience as a leader coach nurtures a deep level of personal development that touches every part of your life, not just your professional world. It can permeate through your relationships as a friend, partner, spouse, parent, mentor, colleague and so on. When you start to listen for deeper meaning you notice different things and so ask different questions, and this can transform your relationship with others and with yourself.

Figure 10.1   Self, others and organization lenses

The 'others' lens, discussed in the second part of the book, can transform relationships at work. An easy start point can be with your own direct reports and team. There are hundreds of moments each day for you to do this. Being a leader coach is about taking the opportunities that already exist and making small changes in how you show up, for example in how you have one-to-one check-ins with your direct reports, the sorts of questions you ask colleagues to shift thinking and how you lead team meetings in a way that includes and encourages every voice in the room (or on the screen). You're now equipped to explore the role you could be playing in any unhelpful dynamics that are creating obstacles for you or your team. You have greater insight into the deeper structure of language and how listening with an inquisitive mind can give you clues about how to shift stuck patterns of thinking or behaviour. Frustration can shift to a sense of freedom and progress in relationships that have previously been at an impasse.

Taking a coaching mindset, skills and behaviours into your role is an opportunity to create a stronger and more sustainable organization, explored through the 'organization' lens in the third and final part of this book. You can play a part in strengthening the coaching culture of your organization so that colleagues feel they are seen and heard and are motivated and engaged at work. If you are fortunate to work in an organization that is investing in a coaching culture you might have broader opportunities, for example to coach future leaders, be a part of mentoring programmes, to shape people processes and align people strategy with business strategy.

'It's not a programme'

I'm often asked if I can share the details of a coaching strategy, leadership development programme or culture initiative that will create a coaching culture. What I've learnt is that something that works in one organization typically won't successfully transport to another. The environment needs to be open to what's being introduced. Integration in organizational strategy and purpose is needed, otherwise the new programme or initiative won't take root enough to shift behaviour. Visible commitment at all levels of leadership is also essential. Leader coaches who role model coaching skills such as deep listening, curiosity and open questions, and create space for many voices to be heard can create a strong foundation.

As you take on more senior roles your opportunity to shape the environment for others grows. The ripples from your actions are bigger. You have more touchpoints in the organization and, whether you realize it or not, people pay more attention to your words, behaviour and choice the more senior you become. They take their steer from you; what you say and what you do, especially in the difficult moments. It's easy to remain open and curious when things are going well, but what about under time pressure? What about when things aren't going well, or when there's a major shift in your industry, or in the world? There are times when you need to take a more directive approach and less of a coaching approach. These are moments when you can adapt your leadership style to what's needed and at the same time continue to listen, ask questions and make space for other's voices.

Who you are is how you lead and coach

How do others experience you? How do they experience themselves in your presence? These are two critical questions to keep asking yourself as you bring coaching skills and behaviours into your everyday leadership. The shift that you make can have a profound impact on people around you, at work and in your wider life. I frequently hear leader coaches talk about how coaching mindset and behaviour has transformed relationships in their family, with friends, as a parent and in their community roles. It's no longer just about learning some skills and doing coaching, it becomes more about being present, authentic and curious in all parts of your life. This deeper shift in who you are – your beliefs and values – is where we started in Chapter 1, and it's where we shall end here. My hope is that you have in your hands a resource to take coaching skills and behaviours into every corner of your organization, and maybe to transform your wider life as well. Enjoy the journey.

APPENDIX

Embracing the leader coach approach: A path to recognition with the Association for Coaching

VICTORIA LEATH

As you've explored throughout this book, adopting a leader coach approach is not just about managing people – it's about empowering them, helping them grow and nurturing their potential. This method transforms the traditional top-down leadership model into one rooted in collaboration, development and continuous feedback.

The Association for Coaching's definition of a leader coach

The Association for Coaching's (AC) definition of a leader coach is

> someone who applies a coaching mindset or coach approach to get the best out of their talent, enable growth for future success and to achieve collective business and team performance. A leader coach inspires and enables others to adapt to constantly changing environments in ways that unleash fresh energy, innovation, and commitment. To strengthen cultures at work for future generations to thrive.[1]

This definition is at the heart of this book, seeing coaching as a key function of leadership. Instead of simply giving directives, leader coaches engage in meaningful conversations, asking questions that prompt reflection, offering guidance that fosters self-reliance and encouraging employees to take ownership of their own development.

The leader becomes a partner in their team's growth journey, empowering them to unlock their full potential.

By fostering this kind of environment, employees feel supported and valued. They're not just doing a job – they're learning, growing and improving. This approach leads to a more motivated and engaged workforce, higher retention rates and stronger team performance. Teams feel confident, competent and invested in, because their leader is invested in them and their success.

The benefits of formal accreditation

The AC offers a unique leader coach accreditation scheme, designed to recognize leaders and managers who adopt a coach approach to elevate team and individual potential. As a leading global professional body dedicated to advancing coaching in the workplace, this scheme sets a pioneering standard for fostering high-performance cultures. It provides an opportunity to benchmark your skills against rigorous professional standards, focusing on the practical application of coaching within your organization rather than theoretical knowledge. Currently, this is the only scheme of its kind in the coaching profession tailored exclusively for leader coaches. Achieving leader coach accreditation means your expertise and dedication are recognized by an esteemed independent professional body. While adopting a leader coach mindset is powerful, gaining formal accreditation adds a layer of credibility and recognition. But beyond the practical skills, formal accreditation offers a range of benefits:

1 **Increased trust:** When you have gained accreditation, your team knows they're working with someone who has undergone assessment against rigorous standards. This builds trust. Employees feel more confident in your ability to guide them effectively.

2 **Professional growth:** Accreditation opens doors for you, signalling to your organization – and to your industry – that you are dedicated to continuous improvement. This commitment to growth often leads to greater opportunities for advancement, as organizations value leaders who prioritize their development.

3 **Enhanced coaching skills:** The journey toward accreditation provides you with the opportunity for reflection, to refine your skills, learn new methodologies and stay up to date with the latest coaching trends. As a result, you're able to offer more meaningful and impactful support to your teams.

4 **Recognition as a thought leader:** Accredited leaders and managers are recognized as experts in their field. This status not only boosts your personal brand but can also position you as a mentor within your organization. By sharing your knowledge and experience, you inspire others to adopt a leader coach mindset, creating a ripple effect of growth across the company.

5 **Organizational impact:** When you embrace a leader coach mindset and gain formal recognition for your efforts, it influences the entire organization. Teams are more productive, engaged and aligned with company goals. The result is a healthier, more dynamic workplace culture that attracts top talent and fosters innovation.

A journey worth taking

The journey to becoming a leader coach requires intention, self-awareness and a deep commitment to the growth of others. Accreditation is not just a badge – it's a testament to that commitment, signalling to everyone, from peers to employees, that you are invested in making a positive impact. For leaders and managers, adopting this approach and earning formal accreditation is a significant career milestone. But more importantly, it's a transformative experience that shapes how you guide others, influence organizational success and leave a lasting legacy of growth and empowerment.

About the Association for Coaching

The Association for Coaching (AC), established in 2002, is a leading independent and not-for-profit professional body dedicated to excellence, mastery and ethics in coaching, worldwide. Our vibrant, diverse community is made up of professional coaches, leader coaches, mentors, training providers, educators, coach supervisors and organizations building coaching cultures. Our vision is to advance the science and practice of coaching and promote a coach approach to leadership so that coaching 'ripples' out in business and society as a key enabler for performance, responsibility and fulfilment.

www.associationforcoaching.com
Advancing coaching in business and society, worldwide

Reference

1 Association for Coaching (nd), Leader coach accreditation, www.associationforcoaching.com/page/what-is-a-leader-coach (archived at https://perma.cc/95CS-TPCC)

INDEX

Looking for another book?

Explore our award-winning books from global business experts in Human Resources, Learning and Development

Scan the code to browse

www.koganpage.com/hr-learning-development

More from Kogan Page

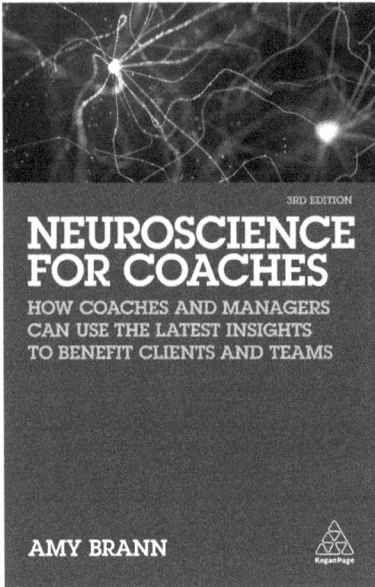

NEUROSCIENCE FOR COACHES

3RD EDITION

HOW COACHES AND MANAGERS CAN USE THE LATEST INSIGHTS TO BENEFIT CLIENTS AND TEAMS

AMY BRANN

ISBN: 9781398604193

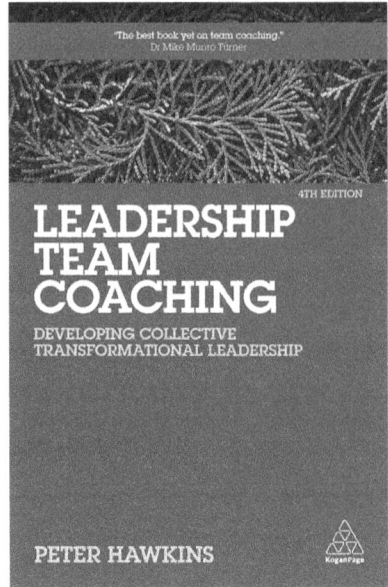

LEADERSHIP TEAM COACHING

4TH EDITION

DEVELOPING COLLECTIVE TRANSFORMATIONAL LEADERSHIP

"The best book yet on team coaching."
Dr Mike Munro Turner

PETER HAWKINS

ISBN: 9781789667455

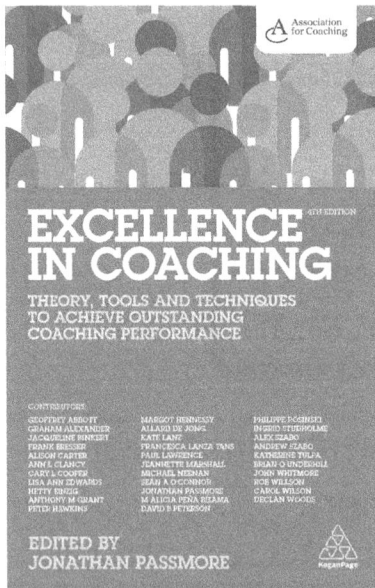

EXCELLENCE IN COACHING

4TH EDITION

THEORY, TOOLS AND TECHNIQUES TO ACHIEVE OUTSTANDING COACHING PERFORMANCE

Association for Coaching

EDITED BY JONATHAN PASSMORE

ISBN: 9781789665475

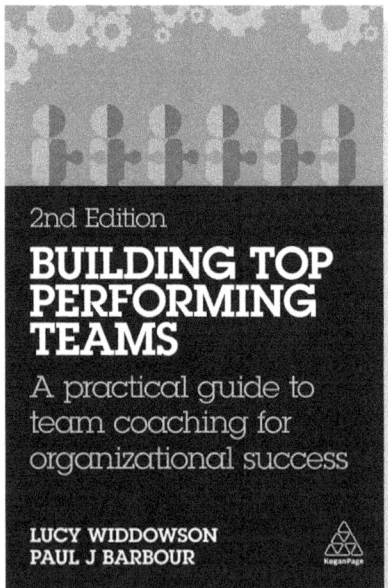

BUILDING TOP PERFORMING TEAMS

2nd Edition

A practical guide to team coaching for organizational success

LUCY WIDDOWSON
PAUL J BARBOUR

ISBN: 9781398620711

www.koganpage.com

From 4 December 2025 the EU Responsible Person (GPSR) is:
eucomply oÜ, Pärnu mnt. 139b – 14, 11317 Tallinn, Estonia
www.eucompliancepartner.com

www.ingramcontent.com/pod-product-compliance
Lightning Source LLC
Chambersburg PA
CBHW061024220326
41597CB00019BB/3328